What Insurance Companies Don't Want You to Know

What Insurance Companies Don't Want You to Know

An Insider Shows You How to Win at Insurance

❖ ❖ ❖

Todd Erkis

Copyright © 2017 Todd Erkis
All rights reserved.

ISBN-13: 9781542320306
ISBN-10: 1542320305
Library of Congress Control Number: 2017900030
CreateSpace Independent Publishing Platform
North Charleston, South Carolina

WHAT INSURANCE COMPANIES DON'T WANT YOU TO KNOW

AN INSIDER SHOWS YOU HOW TO WIN AT INSURANCE

❖ ❖ ❖

Todd Erkis

Copyright © 2017 Todd Erkis
All rights reserved.

ISBN-13: 9781542320306
ISBN-10: 1542320305
Library of Congress Control Number: 2017900030
CreateSpace Independent Publishing Platform
North Charleston, South Carolina

Contents

Preface ·· vii

Chapter 1	Why Does the Insurance Company Need to Know That?	··1
Chapter 2	How to Win at Insurance ························ ·8
Chapter 3	What Type of Insurance Do I Need? ············· 13
Chapter 4	Why Is That Insurance Agent So Friendly? ·········· 26
Chapter 5	Avoid These Common Mistakes ··················· 34
Chapter 6	How Much Life Insurance Do I Need? ············· 47
Chapter 7	I Can't Find Affordable Insurance. Help! ············ 56
Chapter 8	Minimum Car and Homeowner's Insurance Policies Are a Bad Deal ····························· 66
Chapter 9	How to Choose the Right Car and Homeowner's Insurance Deductible ························ 76
Chapter 10	Commonsense Ways to Save on Your Health Insurance ··· 84
Chapter 11	How to Become Wealthy Using Annuities and Life Insurance ································ 99
Chapter 12	The Secret Way to Never Outlive Your Money in Retirement ······························· 113
Chapter 13	An Insurance Action Plan ····················· 128

Glossary of the Common Insurance Terms Used in this Book ····································· 135
Acknowledgements ································· 143
Author Biography ································· 145

Preface

INSURANCE IS COMPLICATED, AND MOST people would understandably prefer not to deal with it. Unfortunately, it's not possible to simply never buy insurance.

Most people think insurance companies are looking to take advantage of their customers and find ways not to pay when people need the money the most.

Insurance company commercials sound convincing, but can you believe what they are telling you? Doesn't it seem like the insurance companies try to make it as confusing as possible?

What if you knew why the insurance companies treat you the way they do and how they figure out the price to charge for insurance? Many people unwittingly do things that lead to overpaying for their insurance, and it's common for consumers to buy insurance products they really don't need. People looking to purchase insurance need to understand what's really going on in a straightforward way, without any sales pitches or fancy marketing language.

I understand the mistrust that many people have with insurance companies. The goal of this book is to provide behind-the-scenes information that insurance companies don't want you to know so that you can be an informed consumer.

Only when you understand what you are buying, how your actions impact what you pay, and what the real price is for insurance do you have a chance to get a fair deal. This book will cover the many types of insurance products that people commonly buy, such as life, disability, car, homeowner's, and long-term care insurance as well as annuity products. The book is designed to help you in all aspects of purchasing, from obtaining a helpful agent to identifying what insurance products you need (and those to avoid) and how to get the best price. The first time an "insurance word or phrase" is used, it will be shown in bold signifying it is in the glossary at the end of the book. The glossary explains these common insurance terms in a straightforward way, without all of that industry jargon.

Insurance is a business, and every business needs to balance making a profit and providing the consumer with a low-cost, quality product. Insurance serves a useful purpose in society, and I will describe in general how insurance products work. Do insurance companies always have your best interests in mind? No, they don't. That being said, sometimes consumers do things that are not in their best interests either, but they don't even know it. I will point out these common mistakes and misconceptions about using and purchasing insurance so that you don't make those mistakes as well.

I am an actuary who worked in the industry for over twenty-five years, although I recently left to teach finance and risk management at St. Joseph's University in Philadelphia, Pennsylvania. An actuary is someone who works with the details of insurance products, and some actuaries determine insurance prices and features. Having worked most of my career in insurance, it upsets me that insurance is so difficult to understand and that many believe it is a scam. When I shop for insurance for myself and my family, I also find the process exasperating—and I have worked for years in the industry! That is why I decided to write this book—as a resource so that people can have the confidence to purchase the insurance they need at a fair and reasonable price.

Although this book will give you advice about how to buy insurance, I am not suggesting you buy any specific product from any specific company. I have no skin in the game about whether or not you purchase insurance. I'm going to try to be general in my descriptions of the products you might buy, and any similarities to actual products from any specific company are totally unintentional. Only *you* can make the decision about what type of insurance you need and how much to purchase, based on your specific circumstances. The goal of this book is to help you make informed decisions about your insurance needs so that you can get the most from your insurance coverage while paying the lowest possible price. Let's get started.

CHAPTER 1

WHY DOES THE INSURANCE COMPANY NEED TO KNOW THAT?

EVERY INSURANCE PURCHASE STARTS WITH the insurance company asking you for a lot of information. The car insurance company will ask: What kind of car do you drive? Where do you live? Who will be driving the car? A life insurance company wants to know about the age, sex, and health of the person who will be covered by the policy.

Insurance companies gather as much information as possible prior to giving you a price and issuing a policy. Are they just looking for ways to charge you more? What are the real reasons insurance companies want to know so many details about you?

To understand how insurance companies use information, pretend that you and your friend Tom decide to go out for dinner at a nice sit-down restaurant where you've never eaten before. You've heard great things about the place, and when you walk in and take a peek around, it seems like the diners are really enjoying their food. It's one price for "all you can eat," but it's not a buffet. In this unique restaurant, you order one dish at a time and must eat the entire serving before you order your next item. Intrigued, you decide to try the restaurant.

You ask the hostess to seat you at a nice table. The server, Paula, comes over and hands you the menu, which lists many interesting dishes. But something is missing: the price for the meal.

After a bit of awkward hesitation, you ask Paula about the price. Paula quickly replies, "Ah, first timers…you've never eaten here before?"

We both nod and say, "No, we have not."

Paula continues, "Can I ask you a few questions please?"

That sounds strange, but you decide to go along to see where it goes.

Paula starts. "Could you please describe how hungry you are?"

Well you're really hungry, and so is Tom, so you both answer, "Very!"

Paula presses on. "When did you eat last, and what did you eat?"

You tell her that you had a sandwich for lunch about six hours ago, and Tom says he had a muffin and coffee as a snack about two hours ago.

Paula says she appreciates your cooperation and asks for a moment. She turns around and quickly walks toward the back of the restaurant. Tom gives you a puzzled look.

Paula returns in a minute or two. Looking at Tom, she says, "Your meal will be twenty-two dollars and twenty-five cents." She then turns to you and says, "Your meal will be thirty dollars, and we can offer you both ten percent off if you eat all of the complimentary bread."

You and Tom laugh out loud and wonder what the heck just happened. Tom asks why there is such a big difference in price, and Paula says she's happy to explain. The restaurant uses a formula to determine the price of the meal that takes into account what a customer weighs (the server estimates each person's weight as they have found that it's embarrassing to ask directly) and when and what the customers have eaten before coming to the restaurant. The restaurant then uses that information to estimate how much each person will eat, multiplies that number by the average cost of preparing the meal (dinner in this case—lunch would be less), adds a little bit for profit and for the risk of charging this way, and voilà, there's the price.

You told Paula that you hadn't eaten for a good amount of time—six hours—and were very hungry. That information and her estimation of your weight put you in the "large-eater" category. Tom was also very hungry but had a snack a few hours ago. That information, along with Paula's estimate of his weight (less than yours), put Tom in the "moderate-eater" category. The restaurant expected that Tom would eat less, so it set the price lower for him than for you. The restaurant estimated how much each person would eat based on the information that it had on each diner. Paula tells you that the restaurant actually has many categories ranging from "small child" to "extra-large eater."

But why did Paula ask whether you had eaten at the restaurant before? Paula explains that the restaurant keeps track of all the customers who eat there. It knows how many times each customer has visited, what the restaurant charged, what each customer ate, and how much money the restaurant made or lost on each meal. When you come to the restaurant again, it uses this information to make a better prediction about how much you'll eat this time, and it helps determine how much to charge for the meal.

If the restaurant didn't make enough money or lost money on your prior visits, it will automatically put you in a higher category (i.e., charge you more) than it would otherwise, and if it made too much, it will put you in a lower category and charge you less (of course, it does not tell the customers if this happens). Then Paula slips in a shocker: "We add an additional fifteen percent onto the price if it's your first time at the restaurant because we're uncertain about how much you might eat." Wow.

You have to ask one more thing, "What about that eating the complimentary bread thing and the ten percent off—that's so random!"

"Well," she says, "it's quite simple. We have done studies and found that people who eat all the bread eat less on average, so that lowers our costs. Lower costs mean we can offer you a discount against our regular price."

The price Paula gave you seems reasonable (even if the way they arrived at it was strange), so you order your first item. You eat until you are full, and the food is really good. As you leave, both you and Tom believe you were charged a fair price for what you ate and decide that you will definitely come again.

So what does this weird restaurant have to do with how insurance companies set prices for insurance? First, just like the owner of the restaurant, at the beginning of the process, the insurance company doesn't know how much of their product you will require. The restaurant uses a few simple questions before you eat to get more information. An insurance company asks many questions, either over the phone or on a written application, when you ask for the price of insurance, commonly called an "insurance-rate quote." These questions have the specific purpose of helping estimate how much of the product (insurance) you will use so the insurance company can estimate how much it expects to pay to you under the insurance policy. The more the restaurant and the insurance company know about you, the more accurate their estimates will be.

This includes your prior behavior. The restaurant uses what you ate at prior visits to arrive at a better estimate; the insurance company does the same by reviewing how many claims you have made in the past. If the insurance company has little information about you or is missing something it deems important, it will increase the price because of the uncertainty. At the restaurant, it seems logical that larger people eat more than smaller people, and adults eat more than children, so it uses that knowledge to charge adults and larger diners more than children and smaller diners. The server asks if you're hungry and when you ate last to get a better view of how much you'll eat this time.

Similarly, each of the insurance company's questions is designed to figure out how much insurance you will use. The goal is not to get everyone's cost exactly right, but to get the *average for each category* as close as possible, so the amount collected in total is as close to the actual costs as possible.

The key to getting a lower price for insurance (also called the insurance "premium") is to get the insurance company to place you in the lowest user category as possible *while telling the truth about your situation and personal circumstances*. Please bear with me while I climb on a soapbox for a short time about telling the truth. It's important to be truthful when dealing with insurance companies. First, lying about your particular circumstances to get a lower price could mean that the insurance company pays you *nothing* if you later have a claim and need the insurance money. If the insurance company finds out that you lied, it may cancel or void your coverage—even if you have a legitimate claim.

Also, lying to an insurance company to get a bigger payout—let's say claiming your roof was damaged after a storm when, in reality, it was already damaged before the storm—is a crime, and you could go to jail. It's called insurance fraud, and it is a big deal. Insurance companies have tremendous resources and experience to catch lies, and make no mistake, they will investigate. This book will provide a number of legitimate ways to save you money and get a fair deal from the insurance companies. You don't need to lie, so please don't do it. It just isn't worth the risk.

The insurance company asks the questions on its application in order to understand more about you so it can estimate how much it expects to pay for insurance claims in the future. It then puts you in a group with other people it thinks will have similar usage or claims. The industry calls this insurance **underwriting** or risk classification. Everyone who drives must have car insurance, so let's take a closer look at that.

When determining your risk category and, therefore, the price, car insurance companies consider your age, what kind of car you drive, and where you live, along with other factors. Studies have shown that young drivers with less experience have more accidents. This means they will make more claims; that's why younger drivers pay more for car insurance than older drivers do. Insurance companies gather information about accident, damage, and theft rates in various locations. They have found that insurance claims vary based on where you live. If you live in a high-traffic or high-crime location, you'll be charged more than someone who lives in a lower-traffic, lower-crime area because you are more likely to have your car stolen or damaged.

So how do you get into the lowest user category possible while telling the truth? Some usage indicators are within your control. Car insurance companies look for indicators of good driving habits, such as students with good grades or drivers with no speeding tickets. People who have a number of speeding tickets are likely drivers who take some risk and, therefore, are more likely to get into an accident (i.e., make more claims) than drivers without any speeding tickets.

If you wanted to be charged less by that all-you-can-eat restaurant, you could have a snack before your meal, which would lower the restaurant's expectation of how much you would eat and thus your cost. You could also eat the complimentary bread, which would cause you to eat less of the entrée and save you 10 percent on your bill.

The *best* way to save is to stop paying for insurance you don't need and use the features of insurance policies to your advantage. This is one of the main goals of this book and will be addressed in many chapters. One example is that many insurance policies have mechanisms called **deductibles** where the owner of the insurance policy shares in the cost of future claims. Although most people believe that deductibles lead to higher costs, they actually lower the cost of insurance coverage and are discussed in detail in chapter nine, "How to Choose the Right Car and Homeowner's Insurance Deductible." Choosing the right deductible can save you serious money on your car and homeowner's insurance.

Insurance companies not only need to estimate how many claims you will make but also how much it will cost when you do make a claim. Our hypothetical restaurant determines how much money to charge in order to cover the total cost of the food by looking at the average cost of preparing the meal they expect you to eat. Since the restaurant doesn't know exactly what you will eat, they use information on the cost of the food they have served on previous nights to arrive at an average cost of the food per person. The theory is pretty simple: if they're right about what and how much diners will eat in total, they will cover their costs on average.

In the same way, insurance companies use the information they have to estimate the cost of the insurance claims you will make. By putting you in groups with other customers it insures, the company arrives at the average cost of expected future insurance payments. So if you drive a Mercedes and get into an accident, the damage will be more expensive to fix than someone who drives a Ford. That's why collision (accident) insurance for a luxury car costs more than for a compact car.

To summarize, insurance companies are looking for information about you to estimate how much insurance you will likely use, meaning, how likely are you to make future claims. They also need to know how much it will cost them when you do make a claim; they also estimate that based on information you provide. Remember to always be truthful about the information you provide to insurance companies. That's not to say that you have to tell them more than what they ask, but if they ask about something specific, tell them the truth, even if it will likely increase the price. A slightly higher cost is worth it compared to losing your coverage or going to jail.

Instead of lying, get rid of unnecessary insurance and wisely choose the features of the insurance you need. You can also take steps to lower the insurance company's expectation about how many claims you will make, such as being careful to obey all traffic laws, or asking about a "good-student discount" if you have children with good grades on your car policy.

There are some surprising ways that people unintentionally put themselves in a higher user category without even knowing it. In the rest of the book, I will show you how to avoid those situations and explain how to present yourself to insurance companies in the best *legal* way possible in order to get the lowest price on all your insurance policies.

CHAPTER 2

HOW TO WIN AT INSURANCE

INSURANCE IS UNLIKE MOST OF the products we buy. When we go to the store and make a purchase, we usually receive something real or tangible in return for our money. For example, a woman walks into Walmart looking to buy a TV, picks a nice flat-screen that costs $498, and walks out with it. She takes it home, plugs it in, and quickly determines whether it works and meets her needs. She then uses it for a while and decides whether or not she got a good deal. But insurance is different. If that same woman buys insurance, she pays money today but walks out of the "insurance store" with only a *promise* of a payment in the future if something (usually bad) happens. Sometimes she will get no money back in return.

Paying for something and getting nothing back seems like she didn't get her money's worth from the insurance company. We all want to get a good product and get our money's worth when we buy insurance. Often though, it's really hard to know if you have gotten a good deal because, unlike the TV, you don't immediately use the insurance after buying it. In fact, you don't know if you will need the insurance policy at all. So how do you know if you got a good deal? This chapter will explain how to "win" at insurance. In this context, winning means getting the right insurance product at a reasonable price and ensuring that you don't make decisions that end up costing you money.

Before we get into winning or losing though, we need to understand what we are trying to accomplish by buying insurance. Many people believe that winning at insurance means getting more money in benefits from the insurance company than what you paid for the policy, or, in other words, making a profit on your insurance coverage. This is a common misconception and misses the fundamental purpose of insurance. Returning to the restaurant example, if people consistently paid less than the cost of the food they ate, the restaurant wouldn't be able to cover its operating costs and would ultimately go out of business. That wouldn't be a good result if you liked eating there. Most diners who liked the restaurant would be happy to cover the cost of preparing the food and providing a reasonable profit to the owners of the restaurant so it could stay in business.

If a majority of the people purchasing a specific insurance product won by receiving more in benefits than what they paid in premiums, either the cost of the insurance would go up dramatically (making it harder to win), or insurance companies would stop selling those types of policies. Insurance companies need to charge a price that pays for the total cost of all claims, plus some money to cover expenses and profit. That doesn't mean I believe insurance companies have the right to huge profits or to deny claims unfairly to earn more money. It's just that if everyone with insurance got more back than they paid in, the entire insurance structure would fail, and no one would be able to purchase insurance.

The fundamental purpose of many types of insurance like life, disability, homeowner's, and car insurance is to help cover the cost of large, unexpected negative financial events that have the possibility of ruining one's finances. For example, life insurance on the main breadwinner of the family helps the family cope with the loss of his or her future income if that person dies. A homeowner's insurance policy helps rebuild a house if it's damaged or destroyed in a storm or fire. In these cases, the goal of purchasing insurance is to protect against what some would call "catastrophic" risks, where a bad event leads to a big financial problem. It would be difficult for single people or families to protect against these types of risks by themselves.

To understand this concept, let's say there was a law that required anyone who wanted to drive a car to have $40,000 in a special bank account. This special bank account would be available to pay for potential future damages the driver might cause in an accident (to people in the other car and to the car itself). The law seems extreme, given that there's only a small chance of a serious car accident. But because we don't know who will have the accident, the only way to be certain those who are hurt will receive compensation is to make sure that *everyone* has enough money saved. Although such a law might work in general, it would make it difficult for most people to afford to drive a car.

Fortunately, this special bank account is not needed because we have insurance companies. The insurance company is paid to cover the risk of driving, thereby benefiting society in general. Instead of making drivers fund individual accounts, states have laws requiring the purchase of car insurance (often called financial responsibility laws). A car insurance company takes the money it collects from its customers and pools it to pay future claims. The insurance company then uses that money to pay the unfortunate people who experience losses. Only a small number of people with losses get paid, which means the majority of people receive no payments from their insurance purchase.

Did the people who received nothing lose? No, they are the *winners*. Yes, they paid the insurance company money and never received a cent back. With a product like a television, spending money and getting nothing for it is a bad deal. But with insurance products like life, disability, homeowner's, and car insurance, getting nothing in return is a victory. Those who didn't use the insurance were fortunate because they didn't experience any catastrophic losses (e.g., they didn't get into any serious car accidents), and, therefore, didn't need the money. The money paid by those who didn't have any losses went to the less fortunate people who did. The insurance worked to help those unfortunate few avoid great financial hardship—something they could not do on their own.

Winning at insurance is buying insurance that protects you from financial ruin at the lowest cost possible. That means you must have enough insurance to be OK if that bad thing happens. If you become disabled for a long time, how much money would you really need to continue to pay your bills? If your house is destroyed in a fire or storm, how much money would you need to rebuild the house and replace its contents? Although thinking about such things might be uncomfortable, you can gain comfort in knowing that your family can still pay its bills if you become disabled or that you can afford to rebuild your house should it burn to the ground.

There are some insurance products where protection from catastrophic risk is not the main goal. **Cash-value life insurance** and annuities are designed to accumulate money for retirement or for estate planning purposes. The specifics of those products are discussed in chapter eleven, "How to Become Wealthy Using Annuities and Life Insurance." Cash-value life insurance and annuities have advantages with respect to federal income taxes because interest earned on money invested with these insurance products is not immediately taxed. The interest is instead taxed down the road (this is called **tax deferral** of interest earnings or **deferral of taxation**) when the money is withdrawn. Similarly, the person who receives life insurance death benefits (the **beneficiary**) doesn't have to pay federal income taxes on the amount received.

When thinking about purchasing insurance to gain a tax benefit, it is important to focus on whether the particular insurance product or annuity is the best way to meet your objective. Specifically, it's important to understand whether the insurance or annuity has some unique feature that you can't get from other sources. Tax-deferral or tax-free features are particularly valuable, and buying products for those purposes might be a great idea. But if you can get the same benefit in another way, it may not be in your best interest to buy insurance or an annuity. For example, using life insurance to save for college-education costs may not be your best alternative when you can open a lower-cost Section 529 education savings plan (named after the section of the IRS code that created the plans), in which no federal income taxes are ever paid if the money is used to pay for education expenses.

Winning with respect to health insurance is difficult to measure. Health insurance is unique as it serves as a discount program for medical services and prescription drug purchases and an insurance policy for catastrophic events. Winning with respect to health insurance is to get comprehensive coverage by paying the lowest cost possible. It's pretty complicated, so I have devoted a whole chapter on health insurance. Heath insurance is discussed in detail in chapter ten, "Commonsense Ways to Save on Your Health Insurance."

Insurance is the only way to protect against unexpected large losses. Focusing on that goal helps you win at insurance by paying the lowest amount for the protection you need. When using insurance products for other purposes, such as accumulating wealth on a tax-deferred basis or passing money to an heir tax free, it's important to make sure that all of the additional costs or fees charged by the insurance company don't eat up the entire benefit. Additional costs are nearly always guaranteed when using insurance in these other ways; sometimes the costs are obvious, and sometimes they aren't.

When considering an insurance or annuity product to build wealth, don't forget the oft-told truisms, "There is no free lunch," and, "If it looks too good to be true, it probably is." Remember that the insurance company is going to determine the average cost of the product so it can recover the amount it'll pay to everyone who buys the policy, plus pay its own expenses and earn some profit. Insurance companies have a lot of expenses to cover, and they'll cover them through fees charged to their customers—in other words, from you! Make sure you understand all those fees before deciding to use insurance products for reasons other than to protect against large, unexpected losses.

CHAPTER 3

What Type of Insurance Do I Need?

To win at insurance, you want protection against the risk of financial ruin at the lowest cost possible. But how do you know what type of insurance you need? The key to determining what insurance you need is to identify where you have significant financial risk if something bad happens. Once you know your risk, you can decide which specific insurance product will best protect you against that particular risk. Taking an honest look at your personal financial situation is one of the best ways to figure out what types of insurance you might need.

If something unfortunate happens to you or a loved one (for example, someone dies or becomes disabled), would there be a serious negative financial impact on you or your family's life moving forward? As I stated in the previous chapter, the primary goal of insurance is to protect against things that have a relatively small chance of happening but would ruin one's finances if they did happen. Identifying those risks is how you determine what insurance you need.

Someone who I have known since I was a child—let's call him Dr. John—had his own medical practice. He made a good living, and he and his family lived a comfortable life. When he was in his late forties, he severely hurt his back and could barely walk. Unfortunately, even after physical therapy and surgery, Dr. John still had significant pain and had to stop working. Several months later, he was still not working as he continued to be in serious pain, and his patients started switching to other doctors.

Dr. John ultimately decided he needed to sell his practice. Although his practice fetched a decent price, nearly all the money from the sale went to pay the doctors and specialists who had treated his back problems. His wife worked, but she didn't earn enough to support him and their two children on her own. Plus, they had the additional expense of his continuing physical therapy and treatment. They could no longer afford their mortgage and were faced with having to sell their house. They were affluent before the injury, but, without his income, they could no longer afford their normal lifestyle. Financially, things were looking bleak.

Fortunately, when he was younger, Dr. John had the foresight to buy a disability insurance policy that paid a significant amount of monthly income in the event that he became disabled. Under the policy, he would continue to receive income every month that he's unable to work until he turns sixty-five. That additional income allowed the family to make it financially, as, sadly, Dr. John was never able to work as a doctor again. The family was spared financial ruin by Dr. John's wisdom in buying disability insurance.

Some of you might think, "I'm not a doctor, and I don't make a doctor's income. Insurance is a luxury I can't afford." But insurance isn't a luxury. The way to keep insurance affordable is to purchase only the insurance you need at the lowest cost possible. Not everyone needs all types of insurance, so I will discuss what type of insurance you need and cover several ways to lower the cost so that the overall cost of protecting you and your family is more affordable. It's not prudent to take a risk (however small) that could financially ruin you or your family. You need to protect yourself against those risks just in case—it's too important not to.

People who skydive always have a backup parachute. Just about every primary parachute works perfectly, gliding the jumper safely to the ground. But the downside of that first parachute not working is huge, so jumpers have a plan in place just in case. You might be thinking, "Well that is why I don't jump out of planes," and I can see your point. The thought of jumping out of a plane doesn't appeal to me either. However, life—not just skydiving—is risky, and awful things, like unexpected back injuries, happen to people every day, even if they try to live as safely as possible.

Wouldn't it be a shame if all your hard work to gain financial stability was lost due to some random event that left you and your family in serious financial hardship? Being sick or injured, losing a valuable asset (like your home), or dealing with the loss of a loved one is bad enough. But not having any or enough insurance can make it almost impossible for your family to recover financially. Insurance is the backup parachute that saves you when that first parachute doesn't open.

Often, insurance companies and agents sell life insurance and annuity products not for insurance protection but as investment opportunities or estate planning tools. It's true that some insurance products have investment features where your money can grow, for example, with interest or have exposure to the stock market. It's also true that there can be tax advantages to purchasing certain life insurance and annuity products. However, using life insurance in this manner is complicated, given that there are often tricky restrictions and tradeoffs. That being said, if you're interested in doing your homework to make sure you understand the ins and outs, there are circumstances where life insurance and annuity products can be useful as an investment or an estate planning tool. These products are discussed in detail in chapter eleven, "How to Become Wealthy Using Annuities and Life Insurance."

Insurance companies don't want you to know that you don't always need insurance. Like any business selling a product, insurance companies want you to believe you need *every type* of insurance. But you only need insurance if it protects against a risk that could leave you in financial peril. The simple questions below will help you identify whether you should buy common insurance products based on your personal circumstances. Consider each question separately for you and your spouse or significant other. Revisit and review these questions again when you've experienced a life event. Life events include getting married or divorced, buying a house, having a child, changing jobs, having a child move out of the house, or retiring. These life events often change a family's financial circumstances, which could lead to needing more or less protection against the unexpected curves life throws us.

Life Insurance

- Would anyone have a serious financial hardship if your income was no longer available?
- Would there be an unaffordable cost to the family to replace the services you provide (child care, for example) if you were no longer able to provide those services?

Buying life insurance you don't need is a waste of money. You've probably seen the television advertisements selling life insurance for young children and babies. Why is that necessary? Nobody is financially dependent upon an infant. Babies are financially dependent on their parents! Therefore, it's the parents who need life insurance in case of *their* untimely death.

Despite the marketing BS, my view is that life insurance should be purchased based on the questions above that focus on financial hardship should someone in the family unexpectedly die. If you answered "yes" to either of the above questions, you need life insurance. If you don't have a spouse, significant other, child, parent, business partner, or some other person who relies on your income, then you don't need life insurance.

Disability Insurance

- Would you or anyone who relies on your income suffer a serious financial hardship if you suddenly had no further employment income for a long period of time due to a disability?
- If you were injured and couldn't work for a few years or more, would you seriously struggle to pay for regular expenses like

food and living expenses *plus* the additional expenses for your care? People who are disabled might have extra costs for things like medical equipment, prescriptions, and home health aides or caregivers.

Insurance companies don't want you to know that researchers have found that during one's working years, the probability of becoming disabled on a long-term basis is significantly greater than dying. Insurance agents would prefer to sell you a life insurance policy because they usually make much more money on life insurance than on disability insurance policies. However, according to the Society of Actuaries (an insurance professional group who studies these things), for people in their working years, the probability of becoming disabled prior to retirement is significantly higher than dying before retirement. For example, for someone who is forty-two years old, the probability of becoming disabled before retirement is approximately 3.5 times higher than the probability of dying.[1] One reason for this statistic, according to the author of the study, is that medical advances have dramatically lowered death rates from serious accidents and illnesses that previously would have been fatal, and those who survive often cannot work while they are injured.

If you answered "yes" to either of the above questions, you need disability insurance. Since most people rely on their incomes to survive, and because the likelihood of becoming disabled during one's working years is higher than premature death, your disability insurance needs should addressed *before* buying life insurance.

But do you need to buy this yourself? Many workers will likely have some disability insurance from their employers. Employer-based disability insurance comes in two forms: short-term and long-term disability insurance. Short-term disability insurance is pretty common and applies when someone is unable to work for up to ninety days. Long-term

---

[1] Stephen Miller, "Where the Individual Disability Market Stands Today," *The Actuary Magazine*, October 2006, https://www.soa.org/Library/Newsletters/The-Actuary-Magazine/2006/October/pub-where-the-individual-disability-market-stands-today.aspx.

disability insurance covers disabilities that cause a person to be unable to work for more than ninety days.

If you don't have enough long-term disability coverage from your employer, then you need to purchase disability insurance. You need long-term disability insurance to replace the income you will no longer be able to earn if you are disabled for a long period of time. A good rule of thumb is to replace 80–90 percent of your current salary. Note that there are limits to how much disability income an insurance company will sell you, so you don't have an incentive not to work. Waiting too long to purchase disability insurance is Mistake Number Two in chapter five, "Avoid These Common Mistakes."

LIFE INSURANCE OR AN ANNUITY AS AN INVESTMENT

- Do you have a significant amount of money saved that you feel confident you won't need until retirement?
- Are you already contributing the maximum you can to tax-advantaged savings plans like a 401(k) plan or self-directed IRA (regular or Roth) plans?
- Do you consider yourself a sophisticated investor?

If you answered "yes" to *all three* of these questions, you might want to consider purchasing life insurance or an annuity as an investment. Life insurance and annuities are a way to save for retirement on a tax-advantaged basis, but they often have significant costs that may make them less attractive than other retirement savings products. If your employer offers a retirement savings plan like a 401(k) with a matching contribution, you're almost certainly better off putting money into your employer's plan than investing it in an investment product offered by an insurance company.

Many financial experts dislike using insurance and annuities as investment products because they aren't always appropriate and can have many hidden fees and expenses. I agree that these products are expensive, but some products have valuable guarantees and can be good additions to a sophisticated investor's retirement portfolio, if used correctly. See chapter eleven, "How to Become Wealthy Using Annuities and Life Insurance" for more information.

Annuities for Retirement Income

- Are you at or near retirement and are worried about possibly outliving your money during retirement?

An **income annuity** is a type of annuity that is designed to provide money on a monthly basis lasting an entire lifetime. An income annuity is different from a **deferred annuity** which is the type of annuity marketed on TV, designed to accumulate money for retirement. Unfortunately, income annuities are hardly marketed at all. If you answered "yes" to the question above, you should consider an income annuity. Income annuities are the best way to ensure you have money during retirement that lasts as long as you live. Income annuities are discussed in chapter twelve, "The Secret Way to Never Outlive Your Money in Retirement."

Car and Homeowner's Insurance

- Do you own a car?
- Do you own a house?
- Is there any chance your house might be damaged in a flood or in an earthquake?
- Do you have unique valuables such as expensive jewelry, paintings, or collectables?
- Do you rent and have significant furniture and other household items? Would it be a financial hardship to replace those items if they were damaged, destroyed, or stolen?

If you own a car, every state has financial responsibility laws requiring at least minimum liability car insurance coverage. If you have a car loan, the lender will require you to have collision and comprehensive coverage to protect the value of the car, as the car is collateral for the loan. But minimum insurance coverage is not enough. How to determine the right amount of car insurance is discussed in chapter eight, "Minimum Car and Homeowner's Insurance Policies Are a Bad Deal."

Collision car insurance covers damage to the car from an accident, and comprehensive car coverage will pay for damage to your car from other sources, such as a fallen tree limb. Car insurance also contains medical insurance (if you're hurt in an accident) and liability insurance (if you hurt someone else with your car). Most people who own a car need collision, comprehensive, and liability coverage.

Everyone who owns a house should have homeowner's insurance, given that a house is often the biggest asset in your portfolio. If there is *any* chance your house might be damaged by a flood, I strongly recommend purchasing a separate flood insurance policy, because *your basic homeowner's policy doesn't cover flood damage.* According to the National Flood Insurance Program (part of the Federal Emergency Management Agency or FEMA),[2] more than 20 percent of the people who make a claim for flood damage live outside of a high-risk flood zone. This means that you should buy flood insurance if you live in a moderate-risk flood zone or even in a low-risk zone if your house is near water or could be damaged by flooding. Don't think that federal disaster assistance will be your fallback, as that aid is usually in the form of a loan that needs to be repaid. Err on the side of caution, and buy flood insurance if there is any chance of flood damage. The coverage isn't very expensive and could save you from being homeless.

---

2 "Understanding your risk," Federal Emergency Management Agency, last modified September 27, 2016, https://www.floodsmart.gov/floodsmart/pages/flooding_flood_risks/understanding_your_risk.jsp.

Earthquake damage is also not covered under a standard homeowner's insurance policy. If you live in an earthquake prone area, be sure to obtain earthquake coverage. If you live in a particularly high-risk zone for earthquakes, it might be hard to find insurance coverage. If you're having trouble finding insurance, see chapter seven, "I Can't Find Affordable Insurance. Help!" Homeowner's insurance policies also have **exclusions** (i.e., you won't get reimbursed for your losses) if jewelry and certain expensive items like paintings are damaged or stolen. To get insurance coverage for those items, you need to buy specific coverage in addition to your standard homeowner's insurance policy, called a **rider** or a policy **endorsement**. Compare the price of the additional insurance against any potential recovery before you buy to make sure you're getting value for your money.

Finally, a landlord's insurance policy normally won't cover a renter's personal property, so renters should consider insuring the furniture and other valuables in their homes, unless the furnishings aren't worth much and could be easily replaced. If you rent, experience a fire, and your things are destroyed, you won't collect anything without a renter's insurance policy.

LIABILITY INSURANCE

- Do you have significant assets that you want to protect from a potential future legal judgment?

If you have significant assets, then you'll need additional liability insurance coverage protection from an **umbrella liability policy**. An umbrella liability policy works with your homeowner's and car insurance coverage to protect you from large legal payments if you're found responsible for another's injury, pain and suffering, or death. This might happen if someone suffers an injury on your property (say a neighbor falls on your icy sidewalk or gets bitten by your pit bull, Fluffy) or if you are at fault in a car accident and are sued for damages that exceed your car insurance **limits**.

Long-Term Care Insurance

- Are you age fifty or older?
- Are you concerned that you'll need to pay someone to take care of you in the later years of your life?
- Would it be a financial burden to pay for that care when you're older and might need long-term care?

Long-term care insurance is designed to pay caregiving and living expenses for people who can no longer take care of themselves. Although most sales of these policies are to people over the age of sixty, some insurance professionals suggest people in their fifties should consider purchasing long-term care insurance as well.[3] Assisted living and nursing home care is very expensive. Genworth Financial's April 2016 "Cost of Care Survey" reported a median cost of more than $3,600 per month for assisted living, and $6,750 to $7,590 per month for nursing home care.[4] If this type of care is needed over a long period of time, the expense can be astronomical.

Long-term care insurance is a way to protect yourself financially should you need assisted living in the future. However, the insurance has some serious disadvantages. First, if you already have health problems that could lead to a need for long-term care in the future, like Alzheimer's or Parkinson's disease, you will not be able to buy a long-term care policy. Also, if you have a family history of these or similar diseases, you may not be able to purchase a policy, or the premium may be very expensive. Even if you are currently healthy, the premium paid for

---

3 Anne Tergensen, "Mistakes to Avoid When Shopping for Long-Term Care Insurance, How to Pick the Best the Policy for Your Needs and What to Avoid," *The Wall Street Journal*, last modified on April 13, 2014, 4:50p.m. ET, http://www.wsj.com/articles/SB10001424052702304756104579449482245063704.

4 "Cost of Care Survey 2016: Summary of Findings," Genworth Financial, May 5, 2016, https://www.genworth.com/dam/Americas/US/PDFs/Consumer/corporate/131168_050516.pdf.
Monthly nursing home care cost is computed from a daily cost, assuming thirty days in a month.

the policy is not guaranteed to stay the same forever. It can be increased in the future if costs for long-term care increase more than the insurance company expects.

Long-term care policies have many terms and conditions describing exactly when the insurance companies will or won't pay benefits that can make it confusing to know exactly what you are purchasing. If you're concerned you won't have enough money to pay for your care later in life if needed, then long-term care insurance may be something to consider buying. Be sure the benefit is enough to cover the standard of care you need in the future. Those who are financially well-off for retirement likely don't need long-term care insurance. If you have enough assets saved and can pay for possible long-term care expenses yourself, then this insurance is not likely necessary.

HEALTH INSURANCE

* Do you have health insurance?

If you answered "no" to this question, I hope I can convince you to purchase health insurance as soon as possible. Everyone needs health insurance because it acts as a "discount program" for medical expenses. Essentially, health providers and drug companies charge significantly more to those without health insurance than those who have it. This is a strange practice (I don't understand why it's legal) where medical providers charge a superhigh price as a "base" charge, knowing full well they will receive much less from the insurance company. My daughter recently had a procedure where the provider charged $3,250.00 but was willing to accept a paltry $285.73 from the insurance company! The only people who have to pay the superhigh price are those without health insurance.

This practice makes no sense. I believe medical providers should charge everyone the same price no matter how they are paid. It would be like going to a car dealer and being charged a lot more if you paid cash versus getting a car loan. Ridiculous! People paying cash upfront (i.e., those without health insurance) should pay *less*, since the provider gets paid immediately and doesn't have to wait for payment from the insurance company (or have to fill out all of those dastardly forms). I hope some politician reads this and starts the process of outlawing this terrible practice. But since that's the way it is for now at least, you have to have health insurance to get access to the lower prices.

Also, everyone needs health insurance to protect against possible catastrophic expenses and financial ruin. Medical care is very expensive, and even a relatively short stay in the hospital can cost enough to ruin one's finances. A 2009 study published in *The American Journal of Medicine* found that about 30 percent of 2007 bankruptcies in their sample stated that high medical bills were the cause of the bankruptcies, and another 26 percent stated that medical bills significantly contributed to financial difficulties.[5] Having health insurance protects your finances if you or someone in your family is sick or injured in the future. It also gives you access to that discount program so you don't have to pay the outlandish full price for routine medical coverage. *For all of these reasons, health insurance is a must-have, even if you are young and healthy.*

I wish I could clearly state which insurance products are best and recommend that everyone buy them. Although all types of insurance *can* be good to have, not every type of insurance is appropriate for everyone. What's best for you really depends on your individual situation. I only purchase an insurance product if I think it's the best way to protect against a risk I have that could lead to serious financial consequences or when the insurance product has some valuable feature that I need that is not available anywhere else. Focus on the most likely and most severe

---

[5] David U. Himmelstein, Deborah Thorne, Elizabeth Warren, and Steffie Woolhandler, "Medical Bankruptcy in the United States, 2007: Results of a National Study," *The American Journal of Medicine* 122 (2009): 741–46.

risks first. You don't need insurance if there is nothing to protect or if you have other (cheaper) ways of protecting yourself against unwelcome scenarios.

Hoping for the best isn't a good strategy because the reality is that your life can forever change for the worse through no fault of your own. It's important to spend time thinking through what could happen, and then getting the right protection for those possibilities. If, heaven forbid, something terrible happens to you, you and your family won't be financially ruined if you have adequate insurance. *Don't go through life without a backup parachute.*

CHAPTER 4

Why Is That Insurance Agent So Friendly?

WE'VE ALL SEEN THE ADVERTISEMENTS on TV where the friendly, neighborhood insurance agent assists the family needing insurance. They have a great relationship where the agent is there in their time of need and even saves them money in the process. Amazing! The agent seems like their best friend and is obviously a trusted advisor. But is this how it works in reality? Should you trust your insurance agent?

At this point, we have hopefully started to think about what insurance we need, but now need to figure out the best way to purchase it. Often, this process starts by contacting an insurance agent.

Who exactly do insurance agents work for, and how do they get paid? The answer is that insurance agents work for the insurance companies or themselves and *not for you. Insurance companies don't want you to know that most insurance agents only earn money when you buy something, and they earn nothing if you buy nothing.* Agents are not bad people (in fact most of them are great), but it's hard to get good, independent advice about what insurance you need from insurance agents when they have a financial stake (i.e., stand to make money) from your purchase.

The payment the insurance agent receives from the insurance company for selling you insurance is called a **commission**. The commission on a new car or homeowner's insurance policy can range from 8 to 15 percent of the first year's premium, with renewal commission levels of about 2 to 5 percent of the renewal premium amount. The commission percentage on a life insurance policy varies significantly based on the type of policy, but it can be as high as 100 percent of the first year's premium, and commissions on annuities are in the range of 3 to 10 percent of the initial deposit amount.[6] The amount of commission can vary significantly depending on the company, even for the same type of insurance.

An agent who sells insurance for only one company is called a **captive insurance agent,** and an agent who sells insurance for multiple companies is called an **independent insurance agent**. Captive agents work directly for the insurance company; they are normally paid salaries and may also receive commissions or qualify for sales awards when they sell insurance products. The benefit of working with captive agents is that they know the company's products really well (as that is all they sell) and can find the best product for you offered by that company. The downside is that your choices are limited to the products offered by that company, even if another company's product suits your needs better.

Independent agents sell insurance products from many different companies and provide a wider number of options. But because they deal with so many companies, independent agents may not completely understand all of the nuances of every product they sell.

Why do insurance companies pay commissions to their agents? They pay commissions because insurance is a complex product and needs to be explained carefully to the person purchasing the policy. Therefore, agents must identify people who might need insurance and explain to them why they need a particular insurance product. It's a difficult job, as many people have a negative perception of insurance in general and just aren't interested. Insurance agents have to talk about bad things possibly happening and end up facing a good deal of rejection. Therefore, the insurance company pays a commission to incentivize their salespeople to make those difficult sales.

I want to be clear: there is nothing wrong with an insurance agent being paid to assist you with your insurance purchases. It's perfectly

---

[6] "How Much Is That Insurance Agent Making Off Of You?" Nolan Hester, insure.com, last modified April 2, 2010, http://www.insure.com/car insurance/insurance-agent-commissions.html.

legitimate and fair. However, commissions are a hidden cost of buying an insurance or annuity policy, and, when costs are hidden, it can be hard to know if the policy is a good deal. A continuing theme of this book is that an insurance company has to charge enough to cover all of their costs (including commissions) and still make a profit. Therefore, although insurance companies actually make the commission payments, the consumers of insurance (i.e., you) ultimately pay for these commissions over the lifetime of the policy.

Also, there are some agents out there who will sell you insurance that you don't need or that is more expensive than you could find elsewhere just so they can make their commissions or meet their sales goals. So before you buy, you should be confident that you need the insurance, understand exactly what you are buying, and make sure the agent is not trying to steer you to a particular product because it has a high commission that will feather his or her nest.

While it could be an awkward conversation, I recommend discussing commission amounts with your insurance agent *prior to making any purchase. This discussion is vitally important if you are considering purchasing an annuity or cash-value life insurance and making a large initial deposit into the policy.* See chapter eleven, "How to Become Wealthy Using Annuities and Life Insurance" for an explanation of why this conversation is so important. The discussion might be less awkward if you start by saying that you understand that insurance agents need to be paid for their services and that you just want to understand more about how the agent would be paid for the various products you are considering. If the agent is only presenting high-commission products (see the ranges above for some guidelines on reasonable commission percentages), you might want to ask to see some lower commission options or even find a new agent.

Any insurance agents that won't have a thoughtful conversation about commissions or how they are going to be paid are not ones you want to do business with. The best insurance agents will focus on helping you and not on their compensation. The good ones know that having your best interest in mind will lead to more sales and money in the long run through referrals and repeat business. While I recommend knowing how much their commissions are, and low commissions are good, don't misunderstand: I am not recommending that you *only* purchase the product with the lowest commission. It's possible that higher commission products would work better for your circumstances. I'm simply recommending that you understand all of the options available and the cost of each one before you purchase.

I recently visited my life and annuity insurance agent, Joe Super (yes, that's his real name). Joe and I met many, many years ago when I had just graduated from college, and we both worked for the Penn Mutual Insurance Company in Philadelphia. At a company softball game, we starting talking and have had a relationship ever since. He's now an independent agent in his late sixties or early seventies. He has the deep, melodic voice of a long-time smoker that I would love to have if I could find a way to get it without putting my life in danger.

I bought my current life insurance and disability coverage from Joe and have recommended him to numerous family members and friends over the years. My recent visit was prompted by the fact that my wife and I recently became empty nesters now that our youngest child is off to college. I also knew that the **term life insurance** policy that I had bought over ten years ago had a premium guarantee that would expire relatively soon. So I went to Joe thinking I should consider buying another life insurance policy.

I really like talking with Joe about anything (including insurance), as he is easy to talk to and is a straightforward, no-nonsense guy. After he looked up my policy, he told me that the guaranteed premium on my term life insurance policy would remain in place for another three years. He reminded me that I had bought a lot of insurance protection. The policy was for $3 million (purchased a long time ago when I had most of my career ahead of me), and my premium is very low. He said that term life insurance prices are the only thing he's seen in his entire career that have gotten cheaper every year, but given that I'm now twelve years older than when I originally bought the policy, I'm paying much less than I'd pay if I bought a new policy today.

Given the change in my family situation (with my two boys off at college and daughter on her own), he wondered if I should actually *decrease* the amount of my life insurance. "What would your wife do with all of that money? Does she really need it at this point?" The question caught me by surprise, but, after thinking about it for a moment, I realized that he was right. I needed to consider whether my family really required that much life insurance anymore. It was the perfect question to ask.

When I originally bought the policy, my wife had stopped working so she could stay at home to raise our three kids. We had some money saved, but not a lot, and we were relying entirely on my income to pay all of the bills, save for college expenses, and to fund our retirement savings. I had some life insurance coverage from my employer, but it was no longer enough to support our growing family in case its breadwinner—me!—met an untimely demise. With $3 million of coverage (yes, it is a large amount), if the worst did happen, my wife could use the interest earnings for day-to-day expenses. For example, if she earned 4 percent interest each year, she would have $120,000 before taxes per year in interest income. She could then use some of the principal amount (of the $3 million) for other expenses, including college. See chapter six, "How Much Life Insurance Do I Need?" for detailed information about how to choose the right amount of life insurance for your situation.

So even though at the time $3 million seemed like a huge amount of life insurance, it made sense for our situation. Joe recommended I buy term life insurance so that the cost would be reasonable. There were other life insurance products called **whole life insurance** and universal life insurance that include an investment component, but those products required much larger premiums. These types of life insurance policies are discussed in chapter 11, "How to Become Wealthy Using Annuities and Life Insurance." I listened to Joe's recommendation and chose a term life insurance policy with a guaranteed level premium for fifteen years (meaning the amount we paid each year would be the same for fifteen years), given that my youngest child would be close to being out of college at that point. Joe shopped around getting prices from various life insurance companies and found one that charged a reasonable price.

At our recent visit, Joe and I wound up talking about a range of subjects, and, before I knew it, an hour had passed, and I needed to be on my way. Although I ended up not purchasing anything new, I'll go see Joe to buy that new life insurance policy in a few years. Looking back at our conversation, I can see why I've recommended him many times to my friends and family. It's clear that he has my best interest in mind and isn't just there to sell me something. He gives straightforward advice that's easy to understand. In my case, he pointed out that the price I currently pay for my life insurance is low, so I should keep the policy for now and that I should reevaluate the amount of insurance I need moving forward. Of course, he'd like me to buy something, but he didn't try to sell me a policy I didn't need. Yes, he knows I'm an insurance expert, but I'm told by the people I have referred to him that Joe deals with them in the exact same way. I was definitely lucky to meet him so many years ago on that softball field.

But maybe you don't have a "Joe Super" or would rather not deal with an agent. If that sounds like you, you're in luck, as there are ways to buy insurance without an agent. Some companies allow you to purchase insurance through the Internet. There are also websites offering term life insurance that offer to "shop around for you to get the best price" or give you free quotes. Term life insurance lends itself to this type of purchase because each company sells pretty much the same product, and it's easy to compare two policies to each other based on price. Of course, if you're not in great health or have questions about what product is right for you, the impersonal Internet may not be your best bet. Internet purchasing options are available for car insurance as well. Some car insurance companies even advertise that they will compare prices for you with competitors.

Whether you decide to use an agent or try to purchase insurance on your own, getting an independent second opinion might be helpful. I would particularly recommend a second opinion prior to purchasing a cash-value life insurance policy or annuity product as an investment. Many insurance or annuity products include significant financial penalties if you want your money back soon after purchase. A great way to get a second opinion is to hire a certified financial planner to take a look at the product you are thinking of buying. Getting a second opinion might be a bit of a pain, but it's well worth the trouble to avoid the penalty you'd have to pay to get out of the insurance or annuity policy early should you later decide you don't want it.

So should you find your own Joe Super or do your own research on the Internet to purchase insurance? If you know a lot about insurance or have a particular insurance company that you've already decided you want to use, then doing it on your own (on the Internet or with that particular company directly) without an agent can work out fine. It may save you a little bit of money, but, likely, the savings will not be that significant. An independent insurance agent is the best alternative for most people because a good one can explain various products and identify the right product for your situation, which an Internet site is not able to do. A captive agent is also fine if you have decided you want insurance from a specific company. Of course, just as there are lousy people in any job, there are some bad insurance agents out there too. When looking for good agent, remember the following:

- The agent should have significant experience with the product you are considering purchasing and should be someone who you can trust.
- Be a bit skeptical and make sure what's being suggested makes sense to you.
- Make sure the agent is listening to you and identifying products that meet your needs instead of trying to convince you to purchase a specific product.
- Ask about commission levels—if the agent avoids the topic or won't discuss it, consider finding someone else. Everyone deserves to be paid for their services, but the agent should be honest with you about it.

- It's perfectly appropriate to talk to several insurance agents or an independent, certified financial advisor to get different points of view. Ultimately, the more information you have, the better. If your insurance agent is upset by this, then find another insurance agent.

And finally, remember that insurance agents are friendly, not because they're looking for a new friend but because they don't get paid unless you buy insurance from them.

CHAPTER 5

Avoid These Common Mistakes

INSURANCE IS COMPLICATED. IT IS hard to make an informed decision with all of its confusing terms and features. Unfortunately, this sometimes leads to costly mistakes when purchasing insurance products. In this chapter, we're going to discuss how to avoid several common mistakes people make when buying the insurance protection they need.

MISTAKE 1: NOT SHOPPING AROUND FOR THE BEST PRICE

Almost no one walks into a traditional car dealership and pays the sticker price for a car. Most people know that purchasing a car often involves some negotiation, and you have to shop around (and do research online as to what others have paid for the same car) to get a good price. Without comparison shopping, it's impossible to know if the price the dealership is asking for a car is a good one or a bad one. It's the same with insurance; you have to shop around to get the best price.

I know this sounds easier said than done, but it's not hard to shop around for insurance. A good independent insurance agent (or a good insurance website) can identify the companies with the lowest prices, and you won't have to apply multiple times. Some car insurance companies will even shop around for you. Based on some simple questions and your history (history of speeding tickets and prior accidents for car insurance and health history for life insurance), companies will provide price estimates that you can use to identify the lowest cost provider for the insurance coverage you want. Insurance prices vary significantly from company to company, so shopping around for the best price can save you money, and, often, we're talking about serious money.

The key to comparing insurance prices is to make sure you're comparing apples to apples and not apples to oranges. That means making sure that the products you compare provide the exact same insurance coverage. *But insurance companies don't want you to know that with many types of insurance, they try to make their products different from what other companies offer so that it's hard for you to compare their prices to the prices offered by competitors.* Companies worry that if it's too easy to compare prices, then people will just buy from whichever company has the lowest price (which, of course, you would). When there is a competitive marketplace—and the insurance market is very competitive—competing only on price makes it hard to make a profit. Before you start cursing insurance companies, realize that this is a tried-and-true business practice in many industries, and you've probably encountered it before but just didn't know it.

Given that it might be difficult to compare the insurance products, how do you effectively compare prices? Start with getting the price for a basic insurance policy without any extras, so you can directly see the price of the insurance product. It's a standard trick for insurance companies (and agents) to add "bells and whistles" to the basic policy to make it harder for the consumer to compare products. You can defeat this strategy by starting with a basic policy first, comparing the prices to find the best deal, and then adding additional items if you want. Ask the insurance company or agent to remove all optional products and to show you the price for each additional option separately.

Another "trick" insurance companies and agents do is to convert the price into a monthly or even daily payment. This is just marketing hocus-pocus to make the (probably expensive) annual price seem more appealing. I always compare insurance products using the price for one year. Obviously, you can compare the daily or monthly prices as long as every product is on the same basis. Note that some insurance companies might give you a discount if the payment is automatically deducted from a bank account or add processing fees or other charges to some payment methods. Again, these discounts and fees can make comparisons difficult and offer another reason why I like to use the annual cost for comparison shopping. You can always determine how often you will pay for the insurance after figuring out the best deal.

For some types of insurance, such as car, homeowner's and term life insurance, comparing prices is a pretty straightforward exercise because the insurance coverage is rather standard, and you can usually tailor the terms to be exactly the same between different companies' products. Insurance companies call these types of products "commoditized" because prices are easily compared. It's no different from buying a banana or a box of cereal at the grocery store. Commoditized products are great for consumers who are willing to spend a little extra time shopping around.

Cash-value life insurance and deferred annuity products usually are difficult to compare to one another. This is why I would generally recommend these products only to sophisticated investors. Comparing these types of products requires starting with the same initial deposit amount and insurance coverage, if applicable, and evaluating which product has the most value when you are likely to need the money (e.g., at retirement, likely ten to fifteen years after purchase). The insurance company will provide an **illustration** of the policy value in the future by making assumptions for things like interest credited and expense charges. A good insurance agent is critical when shopping around for these types of products. Read chapter eleven, "How to Become Wealthy Using Annuities and Life Insurance" before making any purchase.

What if, during your comparison shopping, you find a great price from some company you never heard of? Should you only buy insurance from the "brand-name" companies? The general answer is that you should purchase from the company with the lowest price even if you have never heard of it before. Of course, you should consider the financial strength rating of the company from one or more of the major credit rating agencies, like Standard & Poor's, Moody's, A.M. Best, or Fitch. An insurance company's rating can be found on the Internet or on the company's website.

Personally, I would choose the company with the lowest price even if that company had a slightly lower rating than its competitors. Definitely stay within the highest ratings (each rating agency has a different scale, but I would generally categorize one of the top two or three ratings as being high enough), but the company doesn't need to have the absolute highest rating to be secure. Insurance is a highly regulated industry, and it's extremely rare for an insurance company to go bankrupt.

While price and features are important, more subjective factors about the company should be considered as well. How is the company's reputation for providing good customer service, ease of doing business, and timely payment of claims? These factors are particularly important for car insurance because you'll have more interaction with the company than with other types of insurance. Often, it is not easy to find independent reviews about how well a particular company provides customer service. Getting recommendations from friends or family and talking with an independent agent are good ways to learn about these subjective factors.

In my experience, most (non-health insurance) insurance companies try to provide decent customer service and are careful to keep their reputation as positive as possible. I exclude health insurance companies from this statement as they have essentially become "gatekeepers," looking to restrict the use and cost of health care. Therefore, they often do not provide great customer service to you or me as our *employers* are their real customers. There is much more about this in chapter ten, "Commonsense Ways to Save on Your Health Insurance."

Make sure you shop around to get the best price. An independent insurance agent should be able to help, or you can reach out to various companies directly yourself. Ask them to give you a price for the basic coverage you need before adding other features so that you can compare prices. Purchase the lowest price policy from a company with one of the higher credit ratings (remember it doesn't have to be the highest) that has been around for a while and has a significant number of policyholders and assets. In your decision, take into account the company's reputation for customer service—particularly for car insurance (and health insurance if you have options)—given that you'll interact with the insurance company on your car and health insurance more often than with other types of insurance.

MISTAKE 2: WAITING TOO LONG TO PURCHASE LIFE AND DISABILITY INSURANCE

As we discussed in chapter three, "What Type of Insurance Do I Need?" not everyone needs life insurance or disability insurance. Life insurance is only needed if others rely on your income, and an individual disability insurance policy is only needed if you are working and don't have adequate coverage at work. Note that you will lose insurance coverage provided by an employer if you change jobs. That being said, many young and healthy people don't consider buying life insurance or believe they don't need disability insurance because they're young and healthy, and the chances of dying or becoming disabled are so remote.

So instead of buying something that will never be used, young people think it's a smarter move to wait until they're older and have a better chance of collecting before they buy such insurance. While this seems to make sense, waiting is a mistake because the worst time to try to buy any insurance product (not just life and disability insurance) is just before you need to use it. *The best time to buy insurance is when you have little chance of using it.* Of course, we only purchase insurance products that are needed.

As we discussed in chapter one, insurance companies figure out what price to charge by estimating how much they will likely pay out on the insurance in the future. The estimate includes the likelihood that you'll need to use the insurance and how much the insurance company will pay on insurance claims. If they believe you're not likely to use the insurance, you'll pay a lower price. If you're young and healthy, life and disability insurance policies are cheap because the insurance company expects only a few people will collect. Young and healthy people are the "small eaters" in our restaurant example.

Older and less healthy people have a much higher probability of making a claim on the insurance, so they have to pay more—sometimes much more. In some cases, the premium can be so high that the insurance coverage is not affordable, or, if you are really unhealthy, you may not be able to get coverage at all, at any price. The bottom line: to get the best price on life and disability insurance, you should buy when your life circumstances dictate a need for coverage, but when you'll not likely use it (i.e., when you are younger and healthy).

You might think there is a flaw in this strategy, as the cost of the insurance is sure to rise as you age. If you get a low price now, then is it really a good deal? The answer is yes, because you can lock in life and disability insurance premiums in for many years at a guaranteed fixed price. For example, term life insurance can be purchased so that you pay the same (level) amount for fifteen, twenty, and even up to thirty years. (In the industry we call this the "level premium period.") Almost every disability insurance policy also has a guaranteed level premium that cannot be increased over the lifetime of the policy. This is different from car, homeowner's, and health insurance policies where the price charged for the insurance is recomputed by the insurance company each year (or every six months in some cases).

What insurance companies don't want you to know is that the price for your current insurance coverage may go down in the future if you stay relatively healthy. Insurance companies group each person into a category (for example, a woman might be classified as a reasonably healthy woman aged forty to forty-five) and use averages to predict how much insurance all the people in that group will need. They then use the information they have on people in that category to determine the price they'll charge to everyone in that group. Of course, over time, as the women in that example age, the insurance company will assume a higher possibility that some in the group will die or become disabled (as people have a higher probability of dying or becoming disabled as they age). However, insurance companies can't predict the future *for any one person* any better than anyone else can, and that's why they make all their predictions using averages for groups. Like the special restaurant using the average cost of a meal, the goal for the insurance company is to get it right on average, as some in the group will use less, and some will use more.

The insurance company doesn't know if you're more or less healthy than average, but you do. If you buy guaranteed premium life and disability insurance when you're younger and healthier, you are now in the driver's seat when it comes to information about your health. If your health gets worse in the future, but not bad enough that you die or become disabled, you should keep paying for the policy because it will be more expensive to buy another policy with the same coverage (because the price of the existing policy is low relative to what the insurance company would charge people currently in poor health).

If your health is excellent or even just better than average, then you should get a quote for the same policy every five years or so from another insurance company to see if the price has decreased. Your insurance agent can give you an idea of if you're likely to save money with a new policy. However, note that making inquiries could be a bit of a hassle, as you'll have to fill out questionnaires again, and, to actually purchase the new life or disability policy, you'll likely need a physical exam and may have to give a blood sample. If you do find that you can get a cheaper policy, *don't stop paying the premium on the original policy until the other policy is approved and in force.*

Recall that when I was talking with my insurance agent Joe Super, he reminded me that term life insurance is the only insurance product he knew of where the prices had actually *decreased* over time. This happened because people in the United States now live longer than they did even just ten years ago due to medical advances in treating deadly diseases like heart and respiratory diseases and cancer.[7] In the industry, we call this an increase in **life expectancy**.

When insurance companies expect people to live longer, the price they charge for pure life insurance, which is what term life insurance is, decreases. Remember, insurance is an incredibly competitive industry. Purchasing when you're healthy doesn't limit your ability to capitalize on

---

7 Stephen Goss, Karen Glenn, Michael Morris, K. Mark Bye, and Felicitie Bell, "Human Longevity and Implications for Social Security Status," *Social Security Administration— Office of the Chief Actuary, Actuarial Note Number 158,* June 2016, https://www.ssa.gov/oact/NOTES/pdf_notes/note158.pdf.

decreases in the price of life insurance, as you can buy a new policy in the future to get a lower rate if you're still healthy. Also, term life insurance policies do not have a penalty (called a **surrender charge**) if you stop paying or lapse the original policy. If your health deteriorates, you simply keep paying for the policy you have.

Don't wait to purchase life and disability insurance. Buy when you are young and healthy, and lock in the price for as long a period of time as you will need the insurance. My twenty-six-year-old daughter, who is working full time and has no disability coverage at work, just bought a wonderful disability insurance policy for herself. Because she's young and healthy, she was able to get a great deal of coverage at a low price that is guaranteed until she turns sixty-five years old. If you're eligible for a lower price in the future because prices go down or your health is better than average for people your age, you can stop paying the premium on that policy and buy another (cheaper) one.

Even if you missed the chance to buy when you were healthy or if you are on the older side, you should still get coverage if you need it. Shop around to get the best price, as insurance companies often treat certain diseases or health issues (like high cholesterol) differently. Prices vary, so it's important to check with several companies. Your insurance agent can help you figure out whether you can get coverage and what it will cost. If you are having trouble finding affordable coverage (in the industry we would call this having an "insurability issue"), chapter seven, "I Can't Find Affordable Insurance. Help!" discusses strategies you can use to find adequate insurance coverage for a reasonable price.

<u>Mistake 3: Buying Life Insurance for a Child</u>

One of the policies most people don't need but is marketed heavily involves a life insurance policy for a child. This type of policy is often called **juvenile life insurance**, which is a type of whole life or cash-value life insurance. This is different than purchasing needed life insurance when a person is young, as, most of the time, very young children don't need life insurance. I wouldn't advise the purchase of a life insurance policy on a young child unless the family relies on the child's income (e.g., the child is a famous actor, sports prodigy, or something along those lines) or there would be a significant financial hardship on the family for some other reason if the child died. The primary goal of purchasing insurance is to protect against unexpected, significant financial loss. The death of a child, while tragic, doesn't bring significant financial hardship for most people.

Juvenile life insurance is marketed as a "good way to save for college," but it is not a good product, as there are much cheaper ways to save money to fund a college education. Juvenile life insurance is loaded with fees and expenses, including charges for administering the policy, the cost of the insurance protection itself, and money for the company to earn a profit. If the insurance protection isn't needed (i.e., your child is not the next Disney superstar), there's no need for life insurance. One good alternative to save for college is a Section 529 education savings plan that doesn't have the high expenses of an insurance policy and provides similar tax deferral of interest earnings if the funds saved are used to pay for college.

Insurance companies make two other questionable claims in their marketing material about juvenile insurance policies: (1) you can lock in low, level life insurance premium now, and (2) buying the insurance will guarantee coverage in the future "if something bad should happen." *What insurance companies don't want you to know is that these claims are, at best, half-truths and are not good reasons to purchase a juvenile life insurance policy.*

Here are the facts. The payment made on a juvenile life insurance policy is level but it is more than what is needed in the early years of the policy. The additional money sits in the policy to pay for the cost of the insurance when the child is older. This extra amount is often called the **cash value** or "cash balance" of the policy. Although you pay a level price for the insurance, the insurance company charges for the insurance based on its expected cost. After a child survives infancy, the probability of dying increases (although for children, the probabilities are extremely small, thank goodness)—so the insurance company has to charge more each year for the insurance protection.

Recall that the price for life insurance coverage has been decreasing for a number of years due to medical advances and general improvements in the health and life expectancies of the population. Therefore for most people, even if the price was indeed locked in, locking in is exactly the opposite of what you want to do, given that prices will go down in the future if life expectancies continue to increase. Also, saying that the price is "locked in" is misleading because on most whole life insurance policies, insurance companies update the price charged for the life insurance component of the policy every year.

The claim of guaranteeing the child to be able to have insurance coverage in the future is also dubious. Life insurance is designed to protect against large financial loss from premature death. However, the death benefit in many juvenile life insurance policies is small (often less than $100,000) which will not be enough coverage to protect against financial ruin when the child grows up. Also, even if we assume that a child gets sick or injured prior to adulthood and therefore can't purchase a new life insurance policy as a young adult, it's unlikely that anyone will rely on the child's income, and, therefore, no large financial loss will occur if that income was no longer available.

The biggest risk to the family is the possible need to provide financial support to the sick or injured child, and the lack of, or decrease in, the child's future earning power due to the sickness or injury. Therefore, disability insurance would really be the best product in this situation, as it would provide income while the sick or injured child (who is now an adult) couldn't work. Unfortunately, disability insurance is limited to replacing one's current income, so it's not possible to get disability insurance on a young child (unless that child is already earning a significant income).

Without a real need for life insurance on a child, you shouldn't buy it just to lock in low rates or so that the child will have insurance protection in the future. Juvenile policies are simply not good deals and shouldn't be bought except in rare circumstances. If a parent or grandparent wants to help with a child's education expenses, a nice gift into a Section 529 education savings plan would be a far better choice.

MISTAKE 4: BUYING UNNECESSARY INSURANCE PRODUCTS

It's important to buy enough insurance, but it's a waste of money to purchase insurance products that are not needed. You should only purchase insurance to protect against unexpected large financial losses or to provide something that can't be gained in some other, cheaper way. It's in the best interest of the insurance company and agent to convince you to buy as many insurance products as possible: more products equals more money for them. One way insurance companies try to sell more products is to sell you additional coverage, called a rider, on an insurance policy.

Riders on life insurance and disability policies are rarely a good value and I don't recommend you buy them. Think of riders as the "extras" offered to you when purchasing a new car from a car dealer. After you've picked out the specific model and settled on a price, the salesperson often talks up other options for your new car, such as undercoating spray, rustproofing, and fabric protection. These extras seem relatively inexpensive (compared to the price of the car that is), and are either unnecessary or things you can do yourself for much less money. They're mainly offered to pad the profits of the dealership. *Insurance companies don't want you to know that they often make a lot of money on the extras and additions they offer you as life insurance and disability riders.*

There are some insurance riders that do have value. A rider or endorsement on a homeowner's policy will cover expensive artwork or jewelry for an additional cost. Also, some riders on annuity products have value and should be considered. As discussed in chapter eleven, "How to Become Wealthy Using Annuities and Life Insurance," **variable annuity** riders are valuable, and no one should purchase a variable annuity without a rider. Of course, as I will discuss later, a variable annuity is a complicated product, packed with expenses and fees and is not something that most people should purchase.

In a similar way to life insurance riders, so-called "specialty" insurance products should also be avoided. Specialty insurance products include credit life, credit disability, burial (sometimes called "final expense" or "preneed" insurance), and travel life insurance. All are bad deals for a variety of reasons. They are commonly sold during stressful times (buying a car or home, after attending a funeral, or planning a trip), so it's hard to make a reasoned decision about whether you need the policy. Often only one company's product is offered, making it impossible to shop around for the best price—a major no-no. Most importantly, although the cost may seem small relative to what you are buying at the time, it turns out they are actually quite expensive relative to the value provided.

You can purchase many specialty insurance products with few, or sometimes no, questions asked. This may sound like a great thing, but it is not. If the company asks you only a few questions (called **limited underwriting**) or no questions at all (called **guaranteed issue**) when you buy the policy, it is a big red flag signaling that the policy is expensive. *What insurance companies don't want you to know is that anytime they offer life insurance without asking for much information, they either think the chance of the event happening that triggers a payment on the policy is remote (travel life insurance) or they are assuming you are unhealthy and will charge a high price (credit life and disability and burial insurance) relative to the benefit provided.*

The insurance company needs information about you to figure out how often you will use your insurance and to determine the correct price to charge. If they have no information, just like in that restaurant example back in chapter one, they'll assume you're a large eater and charge you big-time for the insurance. Or the policy will have significant limitations and exclusions, so anyone who needs the insurance right after purchase will receive little. Often all you'll receive is a refund of the money paid to purchase the policy—in other words, nothing.

Like many "rules," there is an exception. Some insurance companies are starting to sell limited amounts of life insurance (including term life insurance) at their regular price with few questions. The idea is to use all available information on the person applying for insurance including his or her credit score, prescription medicines being taken and items found on social media to estimate the person's health status. If the information found shows no evidence of poor health, the insurance company charges its normal price. If the insurance company finds anything troubling on the person, it will require more information before selling the policy. Insurance companies hope the cost savings from selling policies this way will offset any unexpected increase in benefits paid on these "accelerated underwritten" policies.

There are many other potential traps waiting to take a bit more of your money when you purchase insurance. Various other "add-ons" with names like guaranteed insurability, double indemnity, waiver-of-premium, or return-of-premium riders are representative of the major ones offered. I won't explain each of them here, but they all provide certain benefits only if very specific things happen. Don't buy them.

The way to win at insurance is to protect against risks that have the possibility of ruining your financial situation at the lowest cost possible. Adding additional specialty coverage to any policy increases cost, often for little benefit. This is particularly true for additional insurance products where the insurance company asks for little or no new information. Don't make the mistake of buying any of these insurance products or riders that you don't need, as all they do is pad the bottom line of the insurance company.

CHAPTER 6

How Much Life Insurance Do I Need?

THE MOST COMMON INSURANCE QUESTION I'm asked by my friends, family, and acquaintances is how much insurance they should buy. Most of the time, people know they need a certain type of insurance but have no clue how much is really necessary. Unfortunately, many people determine the amount of insurance they need in a backward way: they start with how much they want to spend, and then determine how much insurance coverage they can purchase with that budget. Insurance agents often encourage this behavior, as their job is to make a sale, and they know people have limited funds to spend. Another common thought is to only get a minimal amount of insurance protection to save money. This often happens when buyers think insurance isn't worth the money. Both strategies can lead to being underinsured, where the insurance protection does not eliminate the potential for financial ruin. It's a real shame when a person has purchased insurance but still ends up having a significant financial hardship if something awful occurs.

To continue the theme of the previous chapters, I want you to win at insurance. Winning means keeping the objective of insurance in mind: protecting against significant financial risk if something bad happens. The key word here is "significant." Most people can cover some level of financial loss, so we're not necessarily looking for the insurance to cover the entire loss. It is a common belief that insurance should cover everything when there is loss, but that's a mistake. As I discussed in chapter two, "How to Win at Insurance," trying to get the insurance company to pay for everything is not a good strategy; it just leads to higher costs. The most important thing is to make sure the amount of insurance *eliminates* any chance of financial ruin due to an unexpected event like a death, accident, or fire. The goal isn't to make money on insurance or have zero out-of-pocket expenses but, rather, for you or your family to be able to carry on financially after a tragedy occurs.

Ultimately, the right amount of insurance protection depends on the type of insurance you're looking to buy and your specific circumstances. Therefore, a separate analysis is required for each type of insurance you need. This chapter discusses how to determine the right amount of life insurance to buy. The most important thing to figure out is how much money you would need to be financially protected if that bad thing happened and how long you need the insurance to protect against this risk. These same concepts should be used when considering most other types of insurance as well, except for insurance and annuities used as investment products. Those products have different considerations and are discussed in chapter eleven, "How to Become Wealthy Using Annuities and Life Insurance."

I was recently talking with a friend of mine—let's call him Pete—who was shopping for life insurance. He was working with an agent who had provided a price quote for a thirty-year term life insurance policy (often called thirty-year term insurance). Thirty-year term insurance is a basic life insurance policy with a guaranteed level premium for thirty years. Term is the type of life insurance I usually recommend since it's easy to compare prices to make sure you get the best deal. Pete is fifty-five years old; his wife, Kristen, is also fifty-five, and they have a sixteen-year-old daughter.

Pete came to me because he wanted to know whether $700,000 was enough life insurance. He originally wanted $1 million, but the premium was higher than he expected, so his agent recommended reducing the insurance amount to make the insurance more affordable. As an aside, when Pete told me this, I was concerned that he didn't have a good agent, as this is a classic example, as I discussed above, of an agent just trying to make the sale instead of working with Pete to meet his insurance needs. Leaving that question aside, I asked him why he originally picked $1 million, and he said there was no real reason other than it felt to him like it was enough insurance. The price for $700,000 of insurance was more affordable, but he wasn't sure that was enough protection.

I get this question a lot and was happy to help. Normally, life insurance is used to provide a future source of income for a spouse to help cover the bills if a main breadwinner dies. When this is the case, I often suggest using a rule of thumb called the "twenty-five-times" or "4 percent" rule. This is not a scientific method but can be helpful in getting a rough idea of how much life insurance you need. You start by determining the additional pretax income the surviving spouse would need each year to be OK financially in the event of the other spouse's untimely death. The income level required could be the lost salary of the person who died, but it might be less because overall expenses might be lower for the remaining spouse. Let's say the income needed is $100,000 per year. The rule of thumb states that you need twenty-five times this income—$2.5 million—of life insurance.

The logic of the twenty-five-times rule is for the recipient to live off of the income generated by the life insurance proceeds without spending down the base amount. This is why the rule of thumb is also called the 4 percent rule, as it assumes that one can earn 4 percent interest (1 ÷ 25 equals 4 percent) from conservatively investing the life insurance proceeds. Although I find this method helpful as a guide, it should not be used as an absolute. This is because if the surviving spouse needs $100,000 today, he or she will need more than that later in life because the price of things inevitably increases due to **inflation**. Also, in a low interest rate environment, there's no guarantee the surviving spouse can earn 4 percent interest on the money, which may mean he or she has less income than is needed. Again, this is just a guide to help identify if a specific amount of life insurance will be enough.

However, when I asked Pete what he was concerned about, it was not providing income for Kristen if he passed away prematurely. In Pete's situation, Kristen had a great job with a good income, and they had a decent amount of money saved for retirement. Pete was worried about paying for his daughter's college and future wedding expenses if he passed away prematurely. They didn't have much saved for her college expenses, and it was important in his culture for the parents of the bride to pay for her wedding when she was ready to get married. Both he and Kristen had a small amount of life insurance ($150,000 each) through work, but he didn't think that was enough.

Next, I asked him why he was considering thirty-year term insurance. Pete replied, "The insurance agent suggested the thirty-year term policy." Did he need life insurance for the next thirty years? Pete thought about my question. In thirty years, he and his wife would be eighty-five, and his daughter would be forty-six. "Now that I think about it," he said, "I don't really need life insurance for thirty years." His daughter would be finished with college by then and hopefully married many years before. He realized that he only needed to protect against his *premature* death, not his eventual death at the end of a normal lifespan.

I had one last question, "Would Kristen have any financial hardship if you passed away after you were both retired?" Pete didn't think so because their retirement savings would be enough to support her if he wasn't there to share retirement with her.

I summarized what he had told me at this point. "You want to make sure you and Kristen have enough money to pay for your daughter's college and wedding if you die before those events happen. You're in a good spot relative to retirement savings and don't need the life insurance proceeds to fill any retirement savings shortfall if you weren't around. You are in much better shape than most people. Your wife can support herself on her income, so that's not a problem either. My first observation is that at this point in your lives, you need both your and Kristen's income, so she needs life insurance just like you do." Pete hadn't thought about what would happen if Kristen died prematurely and agreed that she needed more life insurance so *he* would be protected if she died.

Then Pete and I considered the time period that they needed protection because it's a waste of money to buy insurance for a longer period than you need it. Clearly, the agent's recommendation of a thirty-year policy was out of line given the ages and goals of this couple.

I reminded Pete that life insurance is only needed to protect against the *premature* death of either him or his wife. After talking it out, Pete was confident that a fifteen-year policy would give them enough protection. At that point, their daughter would have graduated from college, and they would have saved for her wedding (or she would be already married).

Pete had another question though. "Wouldn't it be a safer option to buy the thirty-year term life insurance policy, and then just stop paying after fifteen years if I don't need it anymore?" It was a reasonable question, but I told him that doing it that way would be very expensive. When determining the amount to charge for term life insurance, the insurance company must estimate the probability of a person's death over the entire period that the policy's price is guaranteed. With thirty-year term life insurance, this means the insurance company has to charge enough to cover the possibility of Pete's dying over the next thirty years. Since he and his wife were both fifty-five years old, thirty years of protection would run until each of them reached the age of eighty-five. The insurance company knows that as people age, the probability of death increases substantially—so the insurance company's likelihood of having to pay goes up substantially too.

If Pete and his wife each bought a fifteen-year term life insurance policy instead, the insurance company would estimate the probability that they will die over the next fifteen years, or before they are seventy. There is a much lower probability of dying between ages fifty-five and seventy than there is between the ages of fifty-five and eight-five, so the insurance company will charge much less annually for only fifteen years of coverage. If they die after age seventy, they won't get any benefit from the life insurance they paid for, but they don't anticipate needing it then. This illustrates a key point about winning with insurance: your focus should be on protecting against risk, and not collecting on the insurance. The fact that Pete and his wife likely won't get money from the insurance company makes the insurance more affordable. As I will show later, the annual premium for Pete on a fifteen-year term life insurance policy is almost 60 percent lower than the annual premium on a thirty-year term life insurance policy![8]

Now that we determined that both Pete and his wife needed life insurance and that they needed protection for fifteen years, we finally got to the question of how much life insurance to buy. I asked Pete to estimate the cost of college and wedding expenses for his daughter. He conservatively assumed an expensive private college with no financial aid and a large wedding to arrive at a figure of $300,000. Of course that's what it would cost now, and, because nearly everything gets more expensive each year, that number needed to increase a bit. We decided to increase the amount needed by 5 percent each year for ten years, which increased the amount of total life insurance protection Pete and Kristen needed from $300,000 to $500,000.[9] Taking into account the $150,000 of life insurance they already had meant that they each needed $350,000 of additional life insurance.[10]

Pete went back to his insurance agent and asked for the price of a $350,000 fifteen-year term policy for both him and his wife. He was thrilled with the result: the total premium for *both* policies was about $1,700 per year, versus about $4,800 per year for the single $700,000 thirty-year term policy he was going to buy for himself.[11] They would pay almost 65 percent less, and both he and his wife would be covered. This

---

8 Premium rates vary based on the age of the insured person. The savings shown is based on a 65 year-old male. The percentage savings would be less on a younger person.

9 $300,000 × $(1.05)^{10}$ = $488,688 rounded up to $500,000. Since it is not known when the insurance proceeds might be needed, it is not possible to determine the exact right amount. To be the most conservative, Pete could have increased the amount to be equal to the amount needed at the end of fifteen years. In that case, about $625,000 of insurance would be needed.

10 Pete and Kristen would lose the $150,000 of life insurance provided by their work if they changed jobs, so they could have decided to purchase $500,000 of life insurance each just in case.

11 Quotes are illustrative for purposes of showing relative savings and not the ones actually purchased by Pete. The non-underwritten quotes were obtained on June 3, 2016 from https://www.term4sale.com. The numbers shown are the median quote from the seven lowest quotes provided by the website. Quotes were for a thirty-year term for a fifty-five-year-old male with a face amount of $700,000 ($4,839 per year), a fifteen-year term for a fifty-five-year-old male with a face amount of $350,000 ($1,012.50) and

illustrates how you win at insurance. Pay the lowest amount possible to be protected during the time you really need it. Hopefully, Pete and his wife will enjoy a long life together, but, if not, they'll both be financially protected against either of their premature deaths.

Hopefully, your insurance agent will help you decide how much insurance you need and identify appropriate products for you to use to protect your risk. Unfortunately, like what happened with Pete, you might not be able to rely on your insurance agent for good advice. If you're trying to figure out how much life insurance you need and need some additional help or just want to get a second opinion, my recommendation is to hire a certified financial planner.

What you want is a basic, but comprehensive, financial plan that covers all aspects of your finances, such as saving for college and retirement, and a review of your insurance needs. Ask the certified financial planner to show what your family's finances might look like if you or your spouse's income was no longer available at various points in your lifetimes. This analysis will help you identify the amount of life insurance you need. It shouldn't be expensive and doesn't have to be done every year—once, or at most, a few times in your lifetime is likely enough.

My friend Pete's situation was focused on his daughter's education and wedding, but for many people, the financial risk is much broader. Families with younger children should consider child-care costs if one or both spouses pass away and whether the remaining person's income would be able to cover regular costs of day-to-day living, college, other large expenses, and retirement savings for the remaining spouse. Several years ago, I hired a certified financial planner to create a financial plan for me, and I found it interesting and informative. It wasn't expensive and was money well spent. I thought I knew my financial situation quite well, but I learned a thing or two after receiving the report.

It is important that the financial planner you use is qualified to help you with this analysis. Make sure the financial planner is certified by

---

fifty-five-year-old female with a face amount of $350,000 ($705.50). All quotes were preferred, nontobacco.

the CFP Board®. The CFP Board website has a link for finding certified financial planners in your area and even shows any disciplinary action taken against them. According to the CFP Board website "CFP® professionals are held to strict ethical standards to ensure financial planning recommendations are in your best interest. What's more, a CFP® professional must acquire several years of experience related to delivering financial planning services to clients and pass the comprehensive CFP® Certification Exam before they can call themselves a CFP® professional."[12] I would never use anyone who is not certified as a financial planner for important calculations, such as how much insurance you need.

You want an independent view of your situation and not a sales pitch. Most financial planners will try to sell you other things as well; that doesn't necessarily mean you should avoid them. Although their business includes financial plans, many financial planners also work with other professionals who can provide tax-planning and estate-planning advice. But in this situation, we are really only looking for a basic financial plan for a specific price. If you find someone who is trying too hard to sell you other services at your initial meeting, he or she may not be giving you independent analysis, so beware. Please see chapter four, "Why Is That Insurance Agent So Friendly?" Although that chapter describes what to look for in an insurance agent, the same advice applies when hiring a financial planner.

Before moving on, I want to discuss cost. Earlier I said that adequate insurance should be considered a necessity and should be purchased even if it's a significant expense. I strongly believe in that statement, but it is not an absolute. When determining the right amount of insurance for your situation, you also need to consider whether you could still be financially sound with less insurance than what would be ideal. This is particularly true when money is tight and buying insurance will strain

---

12 "Certified Equals Qualified," Certified Financial Planner Board of Standards, accessed December 12, 2016, http://www.letsmakeaplan.org/why-choose-a-cfp-professional.

the family budget. A good financial analysis of your situation will really help with the decision.

When determining how much life insurance you need, take into account what you're trying to protect and how long you will need the insurance protection. Getting some assistance understanding your financial situation from a certified financial planner can help identify possible financial shortfalls if there is a premature death of any of the main income earners in the family. Decide how much insurance protection you need, and keep the price as low as possible by purchasing term life insurance for only the time period that you need the protection. The secret is to fully understand your financial situation, and make sure financial ruin is avoided if the bad thing you are trying to protect against actually happened.

CHAPTER 7

I Can't Find Affordable Insurance. Help!

MANY YEARS AGO, MY WIFE and I decided she needed life insurance. A few years earlier, she had given birth to our first child, and we had another one on the way. She was still working full-time at that point, and we needed her income to pay the bills. One of the questions on the application asked if she was pregnant, and she answered honestly that she was. We were shocked when the insurance company turned down her request for life insurance and told her to reapply after she had the baby. I had no idea that being pregnant would even be relevant, but it was an outright rejection. Fortunately, everything went well with the delivery; she and our son were fine. Shortly after his birth, she reapplied and was approved.

Why insurance companies refuse to provide coverage or will do so only at an outrageous price is widely disliked and not well understood. What's behind their decision? It's all about how insurance prices are determined. Companies must charge a high price, or in some cases will not sell you a policy at all, if you have some characteristic that it believes will likely lead to you using your policy often in the (near) future.

In our case, although a woman dying from pregnancy or childbirth is rare nowadays, it does happen, and the company my wife applied for insurance with didn't want to take that risk or felt it couldn't adequately charge for that possibility. So they asked her to wait until that risk passed, and, when it did, she obtained the life insurance coverage. Of course she could become pregnant in the future, but that's a possibility for just about every woman of childbearing age.

Maybe your house is in an area where the likelihood of flood damage is much higher than average or is in an earthquake zone. Maybe you have some chronic ailment like diabetes or heart disease, or maybe you've recently been seriously injured. These are some reasons you might be considered high-risk or maybe even uninsurable. If this has happened to you or someone you know, it can feel like the insurance company is being unfair.

While consumers hate being turned down when they want to buy insurance or are offered insurance only at ridiculously high prices, it's the insurance company's job to charge enough to cover their expected claims and expenses and to turn a profit. Insurance companies would run into serious financial difficulty or have to charge really high prices if they sold a lot of policies that were used immediately. It would be like a hungry football team coming to that special all-you-can-eat restaurant we talked about in chapter one. The restaurant would have to charge a superhigh price or would certainly lose money.

Insurance companies have to determine their prices based on how much insurance they expect you to use, and if they expect you will use a lot of it, they have to charge you more than people who they expect will use less. I totally understand; however, knowing that is why the insurance companies might refuse to cover you, or will cover you only at an exorbitant cost, provides no comfort to those who need insurance but can't buy it.

Fortunately, there are some ways you might be able to obtain insurance coverage even if you are considered a high risk or uninsurable for some reason. The first thing to do is understand *exactly why* the insurance company expects that you'll use the insurance often. Most insurance companies will give you a reason when they refuse to sell you a policy or when they provide the premium amount (however high) for the coverage.

Back in the late 1990s, I had trouble getting a disability policy. I applied for disability insurance and was shocked when the insurance company refused to sell me a policy. The reason? My back. A few years earlier, I had decided to try a do-it-yourself project and replaced a stone walkway in my front yard. The job required me to dig up many large stones, replace the damaged ones, and reset the new ones. The day after my amateur foray into hardscaping, the severe pain in my lower back and down my leg made me question my decision not to hire a professional. I'd never felt that kind of pain before, and, unfortunately, it was not going away. After a visit to the doctor, an x-ray, and an MRI, I was diagnosed with a herniated disk. Fortunately, the physical therapy was a great help; the pain subsided; and, after a few months, I felt pretty much back to normal. Although I was in significant pain throughout, I only missed a few days of work during that time, as I could control the pain enough to get my work done.

Fast forward to the application for disability insurance. The company wanted information about my general health. With my consent, my doctor sent all my medical records to the company. At that point, my back had been fine for years, so I thought nothing of it. I'd also never missed a significant amount of work due to my back and never went on disability, even when it hurt the most. But neither of these things mattered to the insurance company. To my surprise, the company refused to issue a disability policy to me due to the herniated disk. Given my back problem, even though it was under control, the company determined that the injury gave me a much higher likelihood of becoming disabled in the near future.

The first thing to do if an insurance company won't sell you a policy or charges an exorbitant premium is to try another company. I asked my insurance agent, Joe Super, if other companies might sell me disability insurance even with my back issue. He checked with other companies but could not find one that would sell me a policy, not even if I paid a lot more in premium. The reason was that back injuries are difficult to diagnose and are a common ailment leading to disability. This led to many claims for disability and losses to the insurance companies on their policies. Therefore, many insurance companies were becoming cautious about selling insurance to people with any sort of back problem, even if it had healed.

Although it didn't work for me in this case, it always pays to shop around. Shopping around is particularly effective if the issue is something relatively minor or is on the borderline of indicating to the insurance company that you might use your insurance often. For example, let's assume you're driving and get a speeding ticket for going eighty-five miles per hour in a sixty-five zone. Then a few months later at your next car insurance renewal date, the price for your car insurance goes up significantly. You contact the insurance company to see what happened, and the agent tells you that this last speeding ticket makes four over the last five years, and this ticket counts against you more since it was greater than fifteen miles over the limit. Both these problems led the company to believe that you are at a higher risk of an accident, and it now has to raise your premium.

Does that mean you just have to accept it and pay the higher amount? No, it does not! *Insurance companies don't want you to know that companies use different information and rules to determine their rates, and some may ignore or discount certain bad information about you.* Some other car insurance company might only consider speeding tickets over the past three years and may not treat that last ticket so harshly. Applying different rules, your driving record may look better to that particular company, and, therefore, it would charge you less than your current company (which just raised your rates) does.

The insurance company's actuaries use averages and mathematical techniques to predict how much money the company needs to pay for the expected insurance payouts and to cover other costs and expenses. These calculations are proprietary—meaning they don't share their rules with other insurance companies—and each insurance company develops its own rules. The only way to find these differences is to shop around.

For life and disability insurance, insurance companies gather various types of data about your health to estimate how often you will use your insurance. Like the speeding ticket in the case of car insurance, different life and disability insurance companies may treat the same information differently. Some of the information they use, like cholesterol levels, weight, and high blood pressure, have ranges that vary from company to company. At one company, a cholesterol level of 120 or lower might be needed to get the best rates whereas at another company, it might be 135 or lower. Unfortunately for me, all the companies we tried were concerned about back injuries, and none would sell me a policy.

If you're working, the next step is to try your employer. Many employers will allow you to buy life and/or disability insurance without requiring a physical exam or blood work. Usually, you can only purchase this insurance during the open enrollment period when you choose your other coverage, like health insurance. As we have discussed previously, you'll always get a better price by providing information to show the insurance company you aren't likely to use the insurance in the future (i.e., that you are healthy). But if you aren't in good health or have some condition that would make it problematic to purchase a policy, purchasing insurance from your employer, if it's offered, is usually the best place to buy. It's also usually cheaper than other alternatives because the insurance company knows you are at least healthy enough to be working. I looked into getting disability coverage from my employer, but the amount of additional coverage I could purchase was limited, so I needed to try something else.

Still feeling strongly about needing more disability insurance and looking for other options, Joe and I discussed other possible ways of obtaining coverage. We didn't find any other good options, so we decided on a somewhat unusual strategy: instead of going without additional disability coverage, we asked the company if it would issue the disability policy with an exclusion for my back injury. This meant that if I ever became disabled due to my back problem, the insurance company would not pay my claim. However, if I became disabled *due to any other reason*, the disability insurance would pay as it normally would. The company agreed to issue the policy with the exclusion, and I bought the policy. The price was reasonable since, other than my back, I was in good health.

Obviously, this was not a perfect result, as I would have preferred to get disability insurance without the exclusion. But when there are issues of insurability, like my back problem, tradeoffs will have to be made. In my circumstance, I felt confident that my back pain was under control, and I planned to be careful (i.e., hire a professional the next time) so that I didn't hurt my back again. I believed the probability of being disabled due to my back was low, given that I didn't even miss work when it hurt the most. But there were lots of other ways I might become disabled, and I didn't feel comfortable not having enough disability insurance to protect me and my family. It was a calculated risk because if my back did get worse, I wouldn't be able to collect from that disability policy, but one I was willing to take. The exclusion allowed me to get the insurance I needed.

Please note that this was my personal situation, and purchasing an insurance policy with an exclusion provision won't work well in most cases. An exclusion only works when the problem is limited to one condition that can simply be "carved out," leaving the insurance to cover everything else. Exclusions don't work if you have an issue that impacts your insurability more broadly (for example, if you are looking to purchase disability or life insurance after being diagnosed with a serious disease). However, my situation illustrates that even if there are some issues, you may have options for getting coverage at an affordable price.

Another potential route for those having trouble getting insurance is to reapply when your situation is different or better. This works best when the issue leading to the higher rates is something that will change—like when my wife was pregnant. Note that you should never remain uninsured if you can help it. Even if you believe you can get a better deal if you wait, it's advisable to purchase an expensive policy now, and then look for a new policy in a year or two if things improve. If you're able to get a new policy at a better price later on, you can then cancel the more expensive policy. Never cancel the original policy until the new policy becomes effective. The key is to understand the reason for denial or the high rate so that you know what the issue is that you need to address.

Smoking is a situation that can lead to higher rates for life, disability, and health insurance. Many insurance companies now treat use of any tobacco products as a likely sign of future health problems. That means not just cigarettes but also cigars, chewing tobacco, and possibly even "vaping." If they think it's more likely that you'll have health problems, they'll charge you more for health, disability, and life insurance coverage. The good news is that if you're a smoker who has recently quit, meaning you haven't used any tobacco products for the last twelve months, many companies will now treat you as a nonsmoker.

As I discussed above, companies generally won't offer pregnant women disability or life insurance policies, so women who are considering having a child should buy policies before becoming pregnant or will likely have to wait until after the baby is born to apply for coverage. There are a number of other common situations that could impact the cost for insurance at one point but may not later on. For example, as I discussed above, traffic tickets will generally "wear off" over time. Previous accidents will have less of an impact on car insurance prices if you have been accident free for a number of years. The same holds true for a temporary serious illness, like being hospitalized with the flu. After you recover, your insurability shouldn't be impacted. But note that chronic health issues like heart issues, diabetes, or cancer may always have an impact, or, at the very least, will take much longer before their impact is lessened or eliminated.

If you have shopped around, can't purchase from your employer, and don't have a temporary problem, there are a few other things to try, but they are not ideal solutions. People with certain high-risk issues who cannot get "regular" coverage might be able to purchase insurance from a government-run or government-supported insurer. This is a last resort when you must have insurance but can't get it from any other company. People with a driving-under-the-influence (DUI) conviction and those who live in a flood zone or in an area prone to hurricanes or earthquakes might fall into this category.

Because states make it illegal for people to drive without car insurance, the state's **high-risk pool** will provide car insurance if there is no other option. It's expensive, but there really is little choice. For those who live in flood-prone areas, the good news is that the National Flood Insurance Program (part of the Federal Emergency Management

Agency) provides flood insurance even to those who live in high-risk areas, and it is pretty affordable.[13]

Florida and some other states that are prone to hurricanes or earthquakes have set up government-supported insurers to provide insurance coverage where "regular" insurance companies will not sell policies.[14] Don't just assume that no insurance coverage is available and go without—that's a mistake. Even expensive coverage is better than none, which can wind up costing you way more in the event of an accident or disaster.

Finally, if you definitely need the insurance (see chapter three, "What Type of Insurance Do I Need?") and have nowhere else to turn, you can try to find insurance from any groups in which you are a member, like the American Automobile Association® (AAA), the American Association of Retired Persons® (AARP), religious groups, or even discount grocery chains like Sam's Club® or Costco®. Some of these groups sell insurance policies (usually life insurance) with only a few or no questions asked. That might sound good, but these policies are almost always bad deals. As was discussed in chapter five, "Avoid These Common Mistakes," if the insurance company does not have any information about you, it must severely limit the benefits paid, and the coverage is going to be expensive.

Remember, there is no free lunch, and to stay in business, insurance companies have to collect more in premiums than they pay in claims. If they offered insurance to people who used it right away, they'd go belly up. With these types of policies, if you make a claim within the first two years, you'll likely only get a refund of the payments you already made or only a small portion of the death benefit. Similarly, guaranteed issue

---

13 "Who Do I Contact If I Want to Purchase a Flood Insurance Policy?" Federal Emergency Management Agency, last modified September 27, 2016, https://www.floodsmart.gov/floodsmart/pages/faqs/who-do-i-contact-if-i-want-to-purchase-a-flood insurance-policy.jsp.
14 "Homeowners Insurance, A Toolkit for Consumers," Florida Department of Financial Services, May 11, 2016, http://www.myfloridacfo.com/Division/Consumers/understandingCoverage/Guides/documents/HomeownersToolkit.pdf, page 8.

disability insurance from an association or club will exclude known conditions (a problem you are aware of when you apply), will likely not pay for disabilities incurred soon after purchase, and will have limited total benefits. *Before you purchase any of these types of policies, make sure you understand the exclusions and limitations, and make sure they work for your situation.* It makes no sense to buy an expensive policy that doesn't give you any protection.

By now, you understand that insurance companies have to charge prices that are high enough to pay for expected claims and expenses and to make some profit. If you have health problems, a poor driving record, or own a house in an area where there are frequent catastrophic events (e.g., hurricanes or earthquakes), you may not be able to purchase insurance, or the coverage will be limited and the price will be high. This isn't because the insurance company is being mean or taking advantage of you—it just believes that you'll use your insurance often.

That being said, there are some ways to get better prices and coverage terms. Start by shopping around for insurance to get the best deal, as prices and terms for insurance policies vary widely. This is true for everyone—those who are having a hard time obtaining affordable insurance and those being offered great rates and terms. The insurance company uses a variety of information to estimate how much insurance you will use, and each company develops its own view independently.

Sometimes, you can obtain affordable insurance coverage by waiting until your circumstances change. Waiting can be particularly effective if you had some driving issues a while ago but your driving record has been good recently. Even if there are current issues that you think will improve in the future, you should always buy insurance now, even if it's expensive, to make sure you're protected just in case. Later, when your circumstances improve, you can replace any expensive policies you bought.

Working people with health issues can look to their employers to get life and disability insurance, as many large employers will offer the ability to buy some additional coverage with no or few questions asked. In some situations, you can ask the insurance company to issue a policy with an exclusion, which provides less coverage because the excluded item is not covered but gives you a chance to obtain insurance that covers everything else. If none of those techniques work, you can buy guaranteed issue life and disability insurance policies, high-risk car insurance, and homeowner's insurance policies offered by state-supported insurance companies that are obligated to cover everyone; they will be expensive and may limit benefits, but not getting any coverage could end up costing you more money if something catastrophic happens.

CHAPTER 8

Minimum Car and Homeowner's Insurance Policies Are a Bad Deal

IT WILL COME AS NO surprise that if you own a car or a house, you're required to have insurance. Every state has car insurance financial responsibility laws designed to ensure that drivers have insurance before they are allowed on the road. What may come as a surprise is that this insurance requirement is *to protect the other people involved in any accident, not you*. Similarly, most homeowners have a mortgage, and the bank requires the house be insured for as much as the amount of the mortgage, but, once again, *this is not to protect you, but to protect the bank*. My goal is to make sure *you* are protected. To protect yourself, never settle for only the legally required minimum amount of car or homeowner's insurance.

I'll start by discussing car insurance, and then move to homeowner's insurance later in the chapter. I will also cover a type of insurance called an umbrella liability policy, which provides protection over and above your car insurance or homeowner's insurance policy limits if a court finds you legally liable after someone is hurt or injured in a car accident or at your house.

Car Insurance
Minimum car insurance is advertised as an affordable way to meet one's responsibility under the law. Although it does meet the legal minimum, it simply is not enough insurance for most people. If you skid into a

tree on an icy road and smash up the side of your car, your minimum coverage insurance policy won't pay to fix it. If you can afford to fix the damage yourself, that may not be a problem, but car repairs—even for relatively minor damage—can be expensive. What if an accident leaves your car undrivable, you can't afford to get it repaired, and it's the only way you have to get to school or work? What if you, heaven forbid, hurt someone severely in the accident? *Everyone* needs more than just the legally required car insurance coverage to protect against possible financial difficulties. But what types of coverage do you need, and how do you determine the amount you need to be protected?

Car insurance is really several types of insurance all rolled into one policy. So before we talk about how much car insurance is enough, we have to discuss what a car insurance policy covers. Here are the different types of coverage:

- Collision coverage pays for damage to your car from an accident that is your fault. If the other driver is at fault, his liability coverage pays for your damages.
- Comprehensive coverage pays for damage to your car from some event other than an accident. For example, if a tree falls on your car or if your car is stolen, the comprehensive coverage part of your car insurance policy pays for your loss.
- Liability coverage pays for damage that you or other authorized drivers of your car are responsible for due to a car accident. This could include the damage to the other person's car or compensation to the other driver, passengers in either car, or bystanders who are hurt. Liability coverage includes property damage liability and bodily injury liability.
    - Property damage liability coverage pays for damage to the other person's car or property, such as a fence or tree.
    - Bodily injury liability coverage pays for medical expenses and certain other costs of any people hurt in a car accident that is deemed to be your fault. Note that these people could be passengers in your car or in the other car.

- Medical payment to insureds (also called "Part B") pays for medical and funeral expenses for the insured person and other occupants of the insured's covered car. This part of the policy is designed to pay for medical expenses that your health insurance will not pay for and has a lower **coverage limit** (usually automatically set by the insurance company) than the limit on the liability coverage discussed above.
- Some states and Puerto Rico have no-fault car insurance laws where the bodily injury liability part of your car insurance applies to you and others in your car even if the other person is at fault in the accident.[15]
    - If you live in a no-fault state, then you'll buy Personal Injury Protection (PIP) coverage, which is also sometimes called No-Fault Insurance. PIP will pay for medical expenses, lost wages, and funeral expenses up to the maximum limits of the policy. You or your passengers may still be able to sue the other driver for additional damages if there are severe injuries; the law varies from state to state.
- Uninsured Motorist/Underinsured Motorist coverage pays for your or your passengers' covered expenses when the other driver is at fault and is either not insured or doesn't have enough insurance coverage (i.e., is underinsured) to pay for damage to you or your property.

Determining the right amount of car insurance coverage means evaluating what each part of the insurance policy is protecting and deciding how much of that risk you can afford to pay yourself. Car insurance coverage each has a different maximum payment amount (called coverage limits or sometimes just limits). I will discuss coverage limits for each of

---

15 As of December 31, 2016, twelve states and Puerto Rico have no-fault auto insurance laws. The states with no-fault insurance laws are Florida, Hawaii, Kansas, Kentucky, Massachusetts, Michigan, Minnesota, New Jersey, New York, North Dakota, Pennsylvania, and Utah. Source: "No-Fault Auto Insurance," *Insurance Information Institute*, accessed January 4, 2017, http://www.iii.org/issue-update/no-fault-auto-insurance.

the three broad types of coverages shown above: damage to your car, your liability in an accident, and uninsured/underinsured motorist protection. Most car insurance policies have other minor features, such as an amount paid for towing expenses, which also have limits, but I won't address them here because most either cannot be changed or are not often changed by the policyholder.

The bare minimum car insurance policies do not include collision and comprehensive coverage. This is because state laws are designed to protect other people from damage, not fix your car. Unless you can afford to fix your car or buy a new one out of your own pocket, collision and comprehensive coverage are must-haves. Collision and comprehensive coverages do not have policy limits, as the insurance company will pay for the damage up to the market value of your car. If your car is "totaled," it means the cost of repair is greater than the market value. At that point, the insurance company will not pay for repairs but will give you money equal to the market value of the totaled car to purchase a similar used car. If you have a car loan, the bank will require you to have collision and comprehensive coverage so that you can repair any damage and can pay off the car loan if the car is totaled.

You may have heard that you don't need collision and comprehensive coverage if you own a car that's not worth much. It's true that you can probably get away with not having collision and comprehensive coverage in that circumstance as long as you have enough money to get a reasonable replacement if the car becomes undrivable. It is important to keep in mind though that the cost of collision and comprehensive is proportional to the value of your car—so if your car is worth little, you pay less—so it might make sense to get the coverage, as it will be quite cheap. Remember that even though your car may not fetch much on the open market, its value to you as transportation is likely much more than the market value.

One of the more important decisions when it comes to collision and comprehensive coverage is the choice of the deductible. The deductible is a dollar amount of the repair that you agree to pay when there is a covered claim. Deductibles lower the cost of insurance because the insurance company will not pay for small damage and will pay less when there is a bigger claim. Deductibles are common in car, homeowner's, and health insurance policies. Please see chapter nine, "How to Choose the Right Car and Homeowner's Insurance Deductible," for more information about how to choose the right deductible.

Choosing the right amount of liability coverage can be a bit tricky. Recall that the liability part of your car insurance pays for your financial responsibility to another person or people you have injured in an accident that is your fault. If you live in a no-fault state, your own liability coverage will pay for medical expenses and other costs should you or your passengers be injured in a car accident. It will also apply, even in a no-fault state, if you are sued by people in the other car(s) who are hurt in the accident and are found liable for damages.

The good news is that cars are becoming safer, with improved airbags and crash-avoidance systems, and most accidents do not result in serious injuries. According to the National Highway Traffic Safety Administration,[16] in the more than six million car accidents nationwide in 2014, 72.3 percent resulted in property damage only (i.e., no reported serious injuries). In the remaining 27.7 percent of car crashes where there were significant injuries, only 29,989 resulted in any fatalities.[17] Looking at it another way, in 2014 there were only 1.08 deaths per one hundred million vehicle miles traveled.

The insurance industry calls this a "low frequency/high severity" risk. This means a devastating (high severity) financial outcome can happen (i.e., you could be liable for severely injuring or killing another person with your car), but the likelihood of that happening is quite small or of a low frequency. Since the chance of the catastrophic thing happening is so small, it can be hard to determine the right amount of

---

16 "Traffic Safety Facts 2014," National Highway Traffic Safety Administration, 2014 National Statistics, accessed December 24, 2016, https://crashstats.nhtsa.dot.gov/Api/Public/ViewPublication/812261.

17 "Fatality Analysis Reporting System (FARS) Encyclopedia," National Highway Traffic Safety Administration, accessed December 24, 2016, http://www-fars.nhtsa.dot.gov/Main/index.aspx.

insurance for these types of risks because it seems like overkill to pay for a lot of insurance protection.

But even though the probability is small, it's important to get enough protection just in case the worst does occur. In an accident where someone is seriously injured or killed, the liability can be large—even in the millions of dollars. That size of a judgment against you likely would be financially devastating. This means our existing assets need to be protected by the liability insurance. In other words, we want the liability coverage in our car insurance to protect against losing our savings and all of our other assets to pay for our liability due to a car accident.

Car insurance liability limits are normally stated as two numbers such as $100,000/$300,000. The first number is the amount of the coverage per person and the second number is the total amount of coverage per accident. For example, let's assume you have $100,000/$300,000 bodily injury liability coverage. If you were at fault in an accident and the other car had a driver and three passengers who were injured in the accident, your car insurance policy would cover a maximum of $100,000 of liability for each passenger, and no more than $300,000 in total due to the accident. You would be personally responsible for paying any amount you are liable for over the $300,000.

Your savings or other assets are at risk every time you drive or let someone use your car. If you have significant assets that you don't want to lose in a lawsuit, then you need higher limits for your liability coverage; on the other hand, if you have limited assets, you can have lower liability coverage limits. The decision should weigh the cost of the insurance against the benefit of having higher coverage limits. Shop around, and get quotes for the rates at various levels of coverage to understand the tradeoffs. Hopefully—and most likely—you'll never need this coverage. But if the unthinkable does happen and you don't have enough protection, you might be plunged into bankruptcy or at least lose a large portion of your net worth. Make sure your insurance protects you from such a disastrous outcome.

For the same reasons, people with a large net worth should strongly consider buying an additional insurance policy called an umbrella liability policy. An umbrella liability policy is a separate insurance policy designed to help pay for large liability awards against you from a car accident, but it could also be from something that happens on your property, like a visitor to your house breaking a leg on your sidewalk because you failed to shovel the walkway.

The umbrella policy will require you to have certain liability coverage limits on your car and homeowner's policies because it works with those policies to provide seamless liability coverage. Your car or homeowner's policy (depending on what happened) would pay first up to its liability coverage limit. At that point, the umbrella policy will pay up to its liability coverage limit. Large umbrella liability policies (it is not uncommon for an umbrella policy to be for $1 million or more) are pretty affordable, and I'd recommend purchasing one if you have significant assets to protect.

Finally, it's common for uninsured and underinsured motorist coverage limits to be the same as the liability limits discussed above. This makes sense because uninsured and underinsured coverage are essentially liability insurance if the other driver is at fault and can't pay. Unfortunately, there are many drivers who either don't have car insurance or don't have enough. If you or someone in your car is significantly injured due to the fault of one of these drivers, then your uninsured and underinsured motorist coverage will pay your losses.

Homeowner's Insurance

Like car insurance, homeowner's insurance insures multiple different things in one policy. Most homeowner's policies cover the following items:

- The house, called a "structure" in insurance language
- Your possessions located on the property
- Expenses you incur if you can no longer live in your house for a period of time
- Your liability to others who are hurt on your property

Expensive items such as jewelry or paintings are not normally covered unless you buy a rider or endorsement to cover them.

Homeowner's insurance covers damage to your house through, for example, fire, wind, or a tree branch crashing into your living room. If one of these things happens, you want to have enough coverage to repair your house to the way it was before the damage, and that means having enough money to rebuild your house if it is totally destroyed. If you have a mortgage, the bank will require you to have enough insurance to at least cover the amount of your mortgage loan. This will protect the *bank's* risk but will not necessarily be enough to rebuild.

The best way to determine how much homeowner's insurance you need is to contact your insurance company. Many companies will help you estimate the right amount of insurance based on rebuilding costs in your local area. At a minimum, you want to have as much insurance as it would cost to rebuild. It's a common mistake to believe that you need insurance to cover the market value of the home. The market value of the house includes the cost of the land and is based on supply and demand. It may or may not be enough insurance to rebuild.

But what if your house isn't destroyed, but your television and furniture in the family room are damaged by a leaking upstairs water pipe? Homeowner's insurance will pay if your possessions are damaged in a covered event. But the amount of money you receive from the insurance company depends on whether you choose a policy that pays the "replacement value" or the "market value" of the damaged items.

Replacement value will give you more money because the insurance company will pay to replace your possessions based on the price to get new items. With market value coverage, you'd only get the current value of the damaged item. The difference between replacement value and market value can be big because many household items lose value quickly. Electronics are notorious for decreasing in value—that sixty-inch big-screen TV that cost $3,000 a few years ago is worth a fraction of that today.

Although you'll get less for market value coverage, you'll pay less for it too. Remember that insurance companies charge based on what they expect to pay out in claims. If you will receive less money when your personal items are damaged, then the cost for that insurance will be lower. Check the cost difference between the two coverages and pick the one that you feel most comfortable with. Some people like the idea of being able to fully replace their possessions with little or no out-of-pocket cost, and choose the replacement value coverage. Other people realize that the insurance won't pay the full cost to replace everything but want to pay less. If the price difference between the two coverages is small and within your budget, then the replacement cost option is best.

When it comes to other coverages such as temporary rental costs or removal of damaged property, there aren't as many choices. These coverages are usually fixed by the insurance company, and the homeowner doesn't usually have the option to modify the coverage limits. Even though you don't have any control over costs or coverages, it's still a good idea to review each of these supplementary coverages to understand what is and is not covered.

Your homeowner's policy also has another important component—liability coverage. This covers your financial obligation to people who are hurt on your property if their injuries are deemed to be your fault. The decision about how much homeowner's liability coverage is needed is similar to the decision about car insurance liability discussed above. Bottom line: if you have significant assets, then you need significant liability protection. If you don't have many assets, then you can get by with lower limits of coverage. And as was discussed above, people with significant assets to protect should purchase an umbrella liability policy. In that case, you'll need to have a certain limit on the liability coverage in your homeowner's insurance to meet the requirements of the umbrella policy.

Finally, if you have jewelry, paintings, or other expensive items, consider buying additional insurance protection on those items. Standard homeowner's insurance will not pay if these types of expensive items are damaged or stolen. Like the restaurant in chapter one that estimated the cost of food on average, insurance companies estimate the amount they might have to pay for possessions based on what the average person has in their house. They don't cover things like expensive jewelry or paintings because most people don't own these items, and it wouldn't be fair to charge everyone for things only a few people have. If you do have something valuable, such as a one-of-a-kind painting or a large investment-grade diamond, you should have it appraised, and buy insurance for the appraisal amount.

Winning at insurance means being protected against financial ruin at the lowest cost possible. People too often focus on paying as little as possible for car and homeowner's insurance, and, therefore, purchase minimum coverage. But minimum coverage protects others involved in a car accident or the bank—not you. Review your car and homeowner's insurance coverages to make sure your coverage limits are adequate so that you can carry on with as little disruption as possible if one of life's many unexpected challenges comes your way.

CHAPTER 9

How to Choose the Right Car and Homeowner's Insurance Deductible

When we consider buying new clothes or new shoes, we know how much we are going to pay before we take them up to the register. Unfortunately, that's not the way it works with most types of insurance. Insurance has a price, but that price isn't necessarily what you'll end up paying in total for the insurance. Many insurance policies have features that end up increasing how much you pay. One example of this is the deductible that is included in every car and homeowner's insurance policy. Common deductible amounts are $250, $500, and $1,000. The deductible decreases the amount you get from the insurance company if you make a claim—in other words, you pay that part of the claim yourself.

Most people hate deductibles. For an example of how a deductible works, let's say you rear-end another car, and your own car needs $10,000 worth of repairs. With a $500 deductible, the car-repair shop will receive $9,500 from your car insurance company when the repairs are made. You have to come up with the additional $500 to pay for the repair. The pain of receiving less than the cost of the repair leads many people to choose as low of a deductible as possible. But is this a good strategy?

One of the problems with a low deductible is that it leads to the mistake of submitting small claims to the insurance company for reimbursement. Often the thought process goes, "I paid good money for this insurance, so I should use it and get some of my money back." But a policyholder who frequently asks the insurance company to pay for minor losses is one the insurance company thinks will use the car insurance more overall. Thus, by making many small claims, you can unintentionally put yourself in the "large-eater" category, when you really want to show the insurance company that you are a "small eater," thereby being charged a lower price.

The more the insurance company expects to pay, the more it has to charge you for the insurance. But there's more. In addition to the money actually paid for each claim, every time an insurance company receives a claim for a car accident (even if it is relatively small), an employee at the company has to review the claim, and the company may have another employee inspect the damage or speak with the car repair shop. Thus, each claim leads to additional expenses incurred by the insurance company over and above just paying for the loss.

In contrast, if the driver paid the small claim, the insurance company wouldn't have to incur any of these other costs for that claim. Of course, a case can be made that any one person's claim won't cause the insurance company to have additional material expenses. But remember that insurance companies have a huge number of policyholders. If most of them paid for small damages themselves, the company's costs would be significantly lower and would lead to lower insurance prices. So the objective of having the insurance company pay for large losses and covering the small losses yourself will help you win by paying less in the long run for the insurance you really need.

This chapter will help you figure out how large a deductible you should select for your car and homeowner's policies. But before doing that, I want to make a few key points about choosing a deductible. It is not possible to know ahead of time which deductible will lead to the lowest cost, because you must choose the deductible amount before you know how many claims you'll have. If you make more or fewer claims than you anticipated, you might have done better by choosing a different deductible amount. But you'll know that only in hindsight. The best anyone can do is make an educated guess to determine which deductible has the greatest likelihood of lowering the total cost of the insurance.

Although consumers generally hate deductibles, insurance companies love them—but probably not for the reasons you think. Deductibles are not evil inventions by insurance companies so that they can charge you more money. The insurance companies benefit in two ways. The total amount an insurer must pay out for claims depends on the number of claims and the size of each claim. As we have already discussed, a larger deductible lowers the amount the insurance company pays when there is a claim.

Deductibles also decrease the overall number of claims because it is much more common for damage to your car or home to be relatively small. In other words, some of the damage will cost less to repair than the deductible. In that case, no claim will ever be filed with the insurance company because the person will just pay for the repair out of his or her own pocket. A larger deductible increases the probability that the damage will be less than the deductible and, therefore, leads to fewer claims than a smaller deductible does. Fewer claims and less paid on each claim leads to lower amounts paid out and directly to lower premiums.

When choosing a deductible, the first thing to consider is how much you can afford to pay to fix whatever damage is caused. Although a larger deductible will get you a smaller premium, you should always pick a deductible where you can afford to pay for the amount not covered by the insurance company yourself every time you have a claim. In the example above, the car needed $10,000 in repairs, but the insurance company only paid $9,500 for the claim. If you don't have the extra $500 available, you can't get your car fixed. Therefore, step one is to only consider deductible amounts you can afford.

Homeowner's policies don't cover damage from floods, hurricanes (named storms), or from earthquakes (also called "earth movement"), so a policy endorsement or additional policy will need to be purchased to cover these risks. Flood, hurricane, and earthquake insurance policies will have different (often larger) deductibles that can be as large as 5–15 percent of the total amount of the coverage provided. This can be a large number, as a 10 percent deductible on a house with $500,000 of coverage is $50,000. If you are in this situation, it is important to understand your financial responsibility if your house is damaged due to a flood, hurricane, or earthquake.

It is possible you will have more than one claim next year, so you need to make sure you can afford the total amount of the deductibles you might have to pay. Since it is not possible to know in advance how many times you will need your car and homeowner's insurance, we will have to make a guess. Use your prior experience to determine a conservative, maximum number of claims that could happen next year. How many times did you make an insurance claim on your car and homeowner's insurance in the last year? How about in any year? Personally, I try to limit the number of claims I make; I've been fortunate to never have made more than one claim in a year on my auto policy, and, to the best of my recollection, I've never had any claims on my homeowner's policy.

Even if you almost never make a claim or only had a few claims in any one year, being conservative is important in this step. The whole point of having insurance is to be able to move on after a bad event happens. You never want to be in a position where you cannot afford to repair your home or car because you cannot afford to pay the deductible. The other thing to remember is to consider *both* your car and homeowner's policies together, as they both have deductible amounts.

Using my situation as an example, to be safe, I would want to be able to come up with the money if I needed my car and homeowner's insurance four times (even though I rarely ever have previously made a claim). In other words, I would only consider selecting a $1,000 deductible if I could afford to come up with $4,000 (4 × $1,000) next year. If money is tight, you may be attracted to a large deductible to lower your premium, but, remember, insurance is to protect you from financial ruin. It's not smart to pay for insurance but still really not be protected. Could you come up with cash to meet the all of the deductibles next year if you needed to? The answer must be yes.

The final step is to calculate what I'm going to call the "breakeven number of claims." Although this may sound intimidating, don't worry about the math, as it only involves subtracting a few numbers, and then dividing. It does involve a bit of shopping around, but it's worth it, as it could save you some money. I'll walk you through all the steps.

However, if you don't want to do any math, and you don't expect many claims next year, a good general rule is to go with the largest deductible you can afford. As noted, insurance companies like it when customers choose larger deductibles, and, in my view, tend to reward a bit more premium savings to customers with large deductibles. Of course, if you use your insurance more or expect a number of claims next year, then a smaller deductible likely will be best.

In order to calculate the breakeven number of claims, you'll need some information from the insurance company. Ask various insurance companies for quotes over a range of affordable deductible levels (for example, $250, $500, and $1,000 deductibles, assuming you can afford the $1,000 deductible). The goal is to compare the premium savings from increasing the deductible to how much more you will have to pay each time you make a claim. This information is used to determine how many claims you would have to make (where you pay the larger deductible) to offset the benefit of the lower premium (from choosing the larger deductible). You can use this value (the breakeven number of claims) to make a decision about which deductible is right for your circumstances.

Let's try this with real numbers using quotes from my car insurance company.[18] Although this example is for car insurance, it would work the same way for homeowner's insurance. To start, I called my car insurance company and asked for the annual premium for my policy with deductibles at $250, $500, and $1,000. The premium with the $500 deductible was $371 lower than the premium with the $250 deductible. The annual premium with the $1,000 deductible was $785 lower than the premium with the $250 deductible.[19] As you can see, moving to a higher deductible can lead to significant savings.

---

18 These quotes are specific to my car insurance policy and should not be used as representative of anyone else's circumstances. Quotes were received by phone on June 7, 2016.

19 Premium differences will vary based on many factors, including the age and sex of the drivers, the number of cars on the insurance policy, and the model and year of the

The breakeven number of claims is the increase in premium divided by the additional amount paid on each claim due to the larger deductible. By "additional amount paid on each claim," I simply mean the difference in the deductible amounts (moving from a $250 to a $500 deductible requires paying $250 more, and moving from a $250 deductible to $1,000 requires paying $750 more). This analysis assumes each claim is greater than $1,000. The numbers are slightly different if some claims are less than $1,000, but it is not material to the overall analysis of which deductible will likely cost you less money.

BREAKEVEN CLAIM CALCULATION FOR INCREASING THE DEDUCTIBLE FROM $250 TO $500

The breakeven number of claims for moving to the $500 deductible from the $250 deductible is:

lower premium with the $500 deductible ÷ difference in deductible

$371 ÷ $250 = 1.48 claims.

In this example, the breakeven number of claims is 1.48 claims of at least $500. Therefore, I would end up paying more in total with the $500 deductible if I make two or more claims greater than $500 in the next year.

BREAKEVEN CLAIM CALCULATION FOR INCREASING THE DEDUCTIBLE FROM $250 TO $1,000

The breakeven number of claims for moving to the $1,000 deductible from the $250 deductible is:

---

cars. These premium rates are unique to my circumstances and should not be relied on by anyone else.

lower premium with $1,000 deductible ÷ difference in deductible

$785 ÷ $750 = 1.05 claims.

In this example, it would be about the same financially if I make one claim greater than $1,000 next year and would end up paying more with the $1,000 deductible if I make two or more claims greater than $1,000 in the next year. The reason it takes fewer claims to breakeven with the $1,000 deductible is because it is more likely to have a claim greater than $500 than it is to have one that is greater than $1,000.

Different people might make different decisions based on the same breakeven claim calculation. If I am pretty confident that I won't make two claims, I could pick the $500 or $1,000 deductible to get a lower premium. Although $785 in annual premium savings is a lot of money, some people might choose the $250 deductible because they don't want the risk of having to pay more with the larger deductible if they do have multiple claims. There is really no right or wrong here. It's just good to make an informed decision.

Keep in mind that if you choose a larger deductible, you'll be less likely to use the insurance because you should only report damage to the insurance company that is greater than the deductible. Since I am focused on protecting against a really bad event like my car being totaled, I always choose a relatively large deductible on my car or homeowner's insurance because I pay for small damage myself—even if the damage is a bit more than the deductible.

To choose the right deductible, you must consider your personal situation. Can you afford to pay the higher deductible if you chose one to get the benefit of a lower premium? It is important not to set the deductible higher than you can afford. It makes no sense to save on the premium but not be able to fix your car or house if it's damaged. Car repairs are expensive. I slowly backed into a pole in my Acura (I couldn't have been going more than five miles per hour), cracked my bumper, and the damage was $1,200. I paid for it myself, as it was only a small amount above my $1,000 deductible. I felt so stupid that I didn't see that pole! But such things like this happen to people every day. Take the time to make sure that, in addition to feeling stupid, you don't also end up having to take the bus.

CHAPTER 10

Commonsense Ways to Save on Your Health Insurance

SEVERAL YEARS AGO, MY FAMILY dealt with a frustrating situation that is, unfortunately, way too common. During his freshman year, my son got sick unexpectedly and had to go to the emergency room when he was away at college. Thank goodness, he was fine. The frustrating part was that several months later, we received a bill from the hospital for $750 stating that a charge by the hospital was not covered by my insurance, and we had to pay. My wife had saved the documentation the insurance company sent us (thanks, dear!) about my son's visit to the hospital. It showed that the cost for the doctor's examination and the medicine he received were covered, but it didn't show the hospital charge. It made no sense that somehow the hospital cost was not covered when everything else from his visit was.

I called the insurance company and was told that it was a snafu in how the hospital sent in the paperwork and not the insurance company's fault. OK, I thought, I'll just call the hospital and straighten it out. I talked with a nice woman who said she would refile the paperwork and that it should be fine. Wow, so easy (I thought at the time). However, more than six months later, we received another bill from the hospital, this time for $1,050. The bill showed the original $750 charge plus some mystery "administrative fee," which I suspected was its version of a late charge.

I called the insurance company again. The person I spoke with said the hospital never refiled the claim, but that the insurance would pay for the charges as soon as the paperwork was received. OK. Back at the hospital, I talked to a new person who said the claim *was* refiled. But, she told me, the insurance company had advised the hospital that they needed some additional information before they could process the claim. Ugh! The woman at the hospital told me that she couldn't provide the information to the insurance company without my son's approval—but he never received any request for approval. My son then called and gave approval to provide the information. What a runaround!

Then, weeks later, it got worse when my son received a notice from a collection agency seeking payment of the $1,050 owed to the hospital. Thinking it was a mistake, I called the hospital, and they said it was their standard procedure to send unpaid bills to a collection agency. I made more phone calls, waited on hold more times than I could count, and the process went on for almost a full year. My son started to receive menacing calls from the collection agency pressuring him to pay the charges. It was hard to continue to hold out, but we refused to pay.

Finally, after speaking with the same person at the insurance company a few times (after a while I figured out to ask for her specifically), she determined the problem was a mistake on their side, as the insurance company didn't realize the hospital visit was during an emergency. They generally wouldn't pay for out-of-network charges (the hospital was in another state, where my son goes to college) but would if it was an emergency. Almost two years later, the hospital finally received payment.

This situation was surreal. I had to walk both the hospital and the insurance company through the problem over and over. The time it cost me was significant, and I felt like the process was devilishly designed to make me pay something that was clearly not my responsibility. Unfortunately, this situation is all too common and affects people everywhere. Why couldn't the hospital and the insurance company work it out between themselves? Why did they refuse to do so and put the burden on me to navigate their impenetrable rules? The hospital made it clear that it just wanted its money and was going to do everything it could to get it. I was even told that it wasn't the hospital's responsibility to deal with the insurance company, and the hospital threatened to send a collection agency after us if we didn't pay (and did).

The insurance company had no interest in helping me figure out what was going on, even though I was its customer. I was incorrectly told *multiple times* that the problem was with how the hospital submitted the claim. When the insurance company figured out its mistake, there was no apology and no "something extra" to help me feel better about the process. In a normal situation, when a company treats you poorly, you stop using that company and take your business elsewhere. But I couldn't do that. I get my insurance coverage, like many people do, from my employer. It was "take it or leave it."

Alienating customers doesn't seem like a good business model, so why does the health insurance company act this way? Because of a simple fact *the insurance company does not want you to know: if you purchase your health insurance through your employer, the employer is the health insurance company's real customer, not you.* Yes, you get the benefit of the health insurance, but your employer negotiates the coverage terms with the insurance company, often pays a significant portion of the premium, and is the one who hires or fires any particular health insurance company. Therefore, the insurance company is really striving to please the *employer*, not you. And every employer has to find ways to limit health care costs and essentially hires the insurance company to be the "gatekeeper," limiting the amount the employees get reimbursed from their health insurance.

Health insurance companies are sticklers for following the rules on what is covered and what isn't, because their customers (your employer) want it that way. The employers want to keep health insurance costs within their budgets and, therefore, must limit the amount of money paid out for health insurance coverage. People who buy their health insurance directly from an insurance company have similar issues because the insurance company determines how much to charge, assuming all of the rules are followed. The company knows it will lose money on the policy if the rules are not enforced carefully. I know that doesn't make anyone feel good about their health insurance company, but it explains why it acts the way it does.

Although the situation with my son shows why health insurance can be exasperating to deal with, it is critical to have. Everyone must have health insurance for two main reasons. First, it is really expensive to get medical treatment without insurance. Health insurance acts as a "discount program" where health providers and drug companies charge significantly more to those who don't have insurance. This is a strange practice that, in my humble opinion, should not be legal. It should be cheaper to pay in cash upfront instead of through insurance, not the other way around. Second, it doesn't take more than a few days in the hospital to run up significant costs. Large medical expenses are a leading cause of bankruptcy. Don't let that happen to you. Everyone needs health insurance to protect against financial ruin.

All health insurance plans require the payment of a premium, but the cost of your health insurance is more than just the premium you pay. Health plans usually have **copayments**, **coinsurance**, and deductibles that can increase the cost of the coverage significantly (all of these items, but excluding the premium amount, are called "out-of-pocket costs"). Copayments are amounts paid by the patient directly to the provider when a service is provided. Coinsurance is a percentage of the covered expenses that is paid by the patient (e.g., 20 percent coinsurance means 80 percent of the covered expenses are paid by the insurance company, with the remaining 20 percent paid by the patient).

The deductible in health insurance is a bit different than the deductible in auto and homeowner's insurance. The deductible is the amount the patient must pay *in total* before the insurance company will pay anything at all. As was discussed in the previous chapter, the car and homeowner's insurance deductible is the amount of *each claim* the person with the insurance pays. Health insurance deductibles are measured over the course of one year. At the end of the year, the entire deductible requirement starts again.

The copayments, coinsurance, and deductibles lower the costs paid by the insurance company, thereby lowering the price for the coverage. These additional payments have an element of fairness because the insured person has to pay more if he or she uses more medical services. Health insurance plans with high deductible amounts ("high deductible plans") have become popular as a way for insurance companies and employers to keep costs and prices down. A main goal of a high deductible plan is to give the patient an incentive to use less medical services because the patient has to pay all of the costs until the deductible amount is satisfied.

The overall cost of a high deductible plan can be quite large. The IRS defines a high deductible plan in 2017 as having at deductible of *not less* than $1,300 for an individual or $2,600 for family coverage.[20] The maximum out-of-pocket cost must not exceed $6,550 for an individual and $13,100 for family coverage. Although many plans have lower maximum out-of-pocket costs than the amount shown above, it can still be a lot of money. The downside is that plans with lower deductibles and out-of-pocket costs have larger premiums to offset the impact of the higher cost to the insurance company.

To understand how a high deductible plan works, I'm going to go over an example where a hypothetical Smith family selected a high deductible health plan last year. I want to apologize in advance that this example will include quite a few numbers, but I hope it will be helpful in explaining how these high deductible plans work. Let's assume their family plan has an individual deductible of $4,000, a family deductible of $8,000, an out-of-pocket maximum of $10,000 and a 20 percent coinsurance percentage.[21] I'm going to ignore copayments in this example, as they are relatively small compared to the deductible and coinsurance requirements.

The Smith family consists of Sam; his wife, Sarah; and their only child, Stephan. Unfortunately, earlier in the year, Sarah fell and broke her leg, which led to an emergency room visit, x-rays, and several other visits to doctors. Everything related to the broken leg cost $4,000. The good news is that she has recovered completely. The bad news is that the

---

20 "Rev. Proc. 2016-28," The Internal Revenue Service, accessed December 15, 2016, https://www.irs.gov/pub/irs-drop/rp-16-28.pdf.
21 The plan terms are for example purposes only and are not necessarily representative of an actual plan sold in the market. Plan terms will vary from company to company and type of plan being offered.

family had to pay the entire $4,000 themselves due to Sarah's individual deductible.

The family had other bills for medical services during the year. Sam had medical expenses of $900 and there was an additional $100 paid on behalf of Stephan. These expenses were also paid directly by the Smith family, since each person's expenses were below the $4,000 individual deductible, and the total was less than the family deductible of $8,000. At this point, the Smith family's out-of-pocket cost has been $5,000, the sum of Sarah's $4,000, and Sam's and Stephan's total of $1,000 in medical expenses. Sarah met her individual deductible of $4,000 but Sam and Stephan have not.

Now let's assume that Sarah had further medical expenses when she had to go to urgent care after accidentally hitting her head and getting a concussion (she's obviously having an unlucky year health-wise). This hospital visit resulted in $2,000 of charges. Since Sarah's individual deductible has been met, the insurance company finally starts to pay for her expenses at this point. But, unfortunately, the insurance company does not pay for everything. Until the total out-of-pocket maximum of $10,000 is reached for the family, the insurance company only pays 80 percent of every dollar of expense due to the coinsurance. Therefore, the insurance company pays 80 percent or $1,600 of the $2,000 charges relating to the concussion, and the Smiths pay the remaining $400. At this point, the Smith family has paid a total of $5,400 ($4,000 + $400 + $900 + $100) in addition to the regular premium for the health insurance coverage.

How much the Smiths pay for additional medical expenses moving forward in the current year depends on who needs the medical attention and the cost of the treatment. The insurance company will pay 80 percent of future medical expenses for Sarah, since she has met her individual deductible. However, the insurance company will not pay anything at this point if Sam or Stephan have medical expenses, since they have not paid $4,000 toward their medical expenses, and the family in total has not paid $8,000 for its medical expenses. After the Smith family has paid a total of $8,000, the insurance company will pay 80 percent of all future medical expenses for everyone until the Smiths have paid a total of $10,000 (the out-of-pocket maximum). After the total out-of-pocket maximum has been reached, the insurance company will cover all of the medical expenses.

The takeaway from this example is that a high deductible plan requires some serious financial planning on the part of the insured. Those with limited financial resources need to be aware of the potential obligation and save accordingly to pay for possible future medical expenses. The good news is that the government is here to help (sorry, President Reagan).[22] The federal government gives a tax break to people with high deductible plans in the form of a Health Savings Account (HSA). An HSA allows pretax money to be deposited in a special account to pay for future medical expenses. This saves you money because money in an HSA that is used to pay medical, dental and prescription drug expenses is never subject to federal taxation. For example, if a person is in a 20 percent federal tax bracket and puts $1,000 in an HSA, the entire $1,000 can be used to pay medical expenses (because it is never federally taxed). If the $1,000 were not put in an HSA, federal tax of $200 (20 percent) would have to paid, leaving only $800 to pay for medical expenses.

You should put as much as you can into an HSA every year if you have a high deductible plan. The HSA is designed to be a savings vehicle so that you can afford to pay the high deductible, but, unfortunately, it may not be enough in all cases. The maximum amount allowed to be put into an HSA in calendar year 2017 is limited to $3,400 for individuals and $6,750 for families.[23] Your goal should be to use the HSA to save as much as possible for future medical expenses. If it is not enough, you need to make sure to save additional money to pay for your responsibility under the high deductible plan just in case. Money in an HSA never

---

22 Ronald Reagan famously said, "I've always felt the nine most terrifying words in the English language are: 'I'm from the government, and I'm here to help,'" at a news conference on August 12, 1986. Source: The Public Papers of the President, Ronald Reagan Presidential Library and Museum.

23 "Rev. Proc. 2016–28," The Internal Revenue Service.

expires and doesn't have to be totally used in the year it's deposited, so you cannot put too much into an HSA.

A Flexible Spending Account (FSA) is another option for some people who get their health insurance from their employers. Those with an FSA choose a specific amount of money to be deducted from each paycheck and use that money to pay for medical, dental, and prescription drug expenses. An FSA has the same tax benefits as an HSA; however, unlike an HSA, money in an FSA must be used by the end of the year or the unused amount is forfeited.[24] For that reason, you must be careful about choosing the amount to put into your FSA. The FSA is a good choice for known expenses, such as prescription drug costs or medical procedures that are scheduled in advance.

Another issue that needs to be considered is restrictions on which doctors or hospitals can be used under your health plan. Most insurance companies use "networks" to try to keep down the cost of the health insurance coverage. "In-network" doctors and hospitals agree to accept lower prices with the idea that they will get more business by being in the network. When choosing a health care plan, it is important to know if your normal doctor and any specialists you are seeing or want to see are in the plan's network. Even if the plan allows it, seeing an "out-of-network" doctor or specialist can be expensive.

As the Smith family example above illustrates, it is extremely important to consider all of the payments you are responsible for, such as deductibles, copayments, and coinsurance and not just take the plan with the lowest premium. The individual and family deductible and the coinsurance percentage may require substantial payments to medical providers if you or someone in your family gets sick or injured. The amount the Smiths had to pay might lead you to decide you'd be better off without health insurance, but that is just not true. *Under no circumstances should you go without health insurance coverage.* The example does

---

24 "Flexible Spending Account (FSA)," US Centers for Medicare and Medicaid Services, accessed July 20, 2016, https://www.healthcare.gov/glossary/flexible-spending-account-FSA/.

illustrate, however, why it might be better, in some circumstances, to choose a plan with a larger premium but smaller deductibles.

Health insurance costs can be depressing, but don't despair. There are some techniques that can be used to lower the overall cost of health insurance. Consider the following strategies and tips to help manage the overall cost of your health insurance:

1. Understand the terms of your plan. What type of insurance coverage is it? What are the deductible and coinsurance requirements?

    The best time to get information about your health plan is when you are signing up for next year's coverage. At that time, it is the responsibility of the employer or insurance company to explain all the terms and conditions so you can make an informed decision on which plan is right for your circumstances. If you have choices, make sure you understand the differences between the plans so you can make an informed decision on which is best for your circumstances.

    If you have questions, try to get a response in writing if possible. Never rely on what someone tells you over the phone; always get it in writing unless the issue is covered in the official policy benefits booklet provided by your employer or insurance company. The written contract will usually overrule anything told to you over the phone.

2. Follow all of your health insurance plan's rules and procedures *very carefully*.

    HMO plans require a referral from your primary doctor before you see a specialist, but with a PPO plan, you can see a specialist without a referral. Some doctors and hospitals are a part of the network, and some are not. Different health plans have different requirements, which can dramatically change how much, if anything, the insurance company will pay.

    One of the most common mistakes that costs people money is going to a doctor or hospital that is not covered under their health insurance plan. Know if your insurance will cover the expense *before* you go to a doctor, hospital, or even a blood testing facility. I went for some blood tests recently, but the insurance company did not pay because it was not with an approved testing lab. Expensive lesson learned!

3. If you find a mistake or have any questions about something that was not paid for, make sure to contact the insurance company as soon as possible.

As I learned with my son's emergency room visit at college, dealing with a health insurance company about payments or a denial of claim is often frustrating. Go into the first conversation assuming that the issue will not be settled immediately, and keep notes about all conversations. You will want to write down the date you called the insurance company, who you spoke with, and the responses. Ask the person you speak with to make a note in the file specifically stating what he or she tells you or agrees to do. Make a note to yourself to follow up on a regular basis if things are not resolved—waiting and hoping it goes away usually will not be a successful strategy.

4. If you have a large family, consider keeping your children on your family plan even if they can purchase coverage elsewhere.

Under current insurance law, insurance companies must allow all family members under the age of twenty-seven to remain on a parent's health insurance plan. Previously, most insurance plans only covered family members over the age of twenty-one if they were in college or a dependent. The increased age limit provides people with larger families a chance to save on their health insurance costs, because many family plans charge the same price for a family with two children as they do for families with three or more.

I have three children and a family health insurance plan. When my daughter graduated from college and started her new job, she declined health insurance coverage from her new employer and stayed on my plan. The price of my health insurance would not decrease if she left our plan, so it was cheaper, in total, for our family if she stayed on my plan.

Of course, this may not be possible if your adult child moves to another city or state where your insurance policy doesn't have many participating doctors or hospitals. You need to take into account that the child may have an individual deductible and coinsurance payments. Consider both the price savings and the terms of the new coverage. If a child's individual health plan would have a lower deductible or better terms, it may be beneficial to pick that plan, even if the family in total has a larger monthly premium.

5. When filling prescriptions, always ask for generic drugs, and use a mail-order company if it significantly reduces your copayments.

    Most pharmacies and doctors will automatically prescribe generic drugs, as they are the same medication but without the brand name. Advertising has brainwashed us into believing that brand names are of higher quality, but that's not true with prescription drugs. Generics have the exact same medication in them but at a significantly lower price.

    Also, some insurance plans will dramatically lower your payment if you get your prescriptions through a mail-order firm. It is often a bit of trouble to do so, but the cost savings can be dramatic. Finally, if your prescription drugs are expensive, there may be equally effective cheaper drugs than the one your doctor is prescribing. Ask your doctor if there are any alternatives you could consider.

The following tips are for people with high deductible plans:

6. Put as much money as you can into an HSA if you have a high deductible insurance plan.

    Money deposited into an HSA is never federally taxed, so it is like getting a 20–30 percent discount on medical expenses. Don't worry about putting too much money into an HSA because any money left over at the end of the year will be available next year, and interest earned on money in an HSA is not taxed.

There are yearly maximum contribution limits imposed by the IRS, but take full advantage of the HSA by contributing as much money as you can.

7. Consider the timing of medical expenses, particularly toward the end of the plan year.

    It is good to keep track of where you are with the individual and family deductibles during the year. Under high deductible plans, you pay until the deductible is fulfilled and much less after. If you can control the timing of certain treatments, you may want to take into account how much of your deductible you have left to satisfy.

    If you are close to or have satisfied the deductible, then you will only have to pay for the coinsurance requirement for all additional medical expenses in that year. If you have any medical expenses coming up that you can move, load up on those expenses in the current year if possible so that the insurance company will pay more. On the other hand, if you have not satisfied the deductible, it might make financial sense to delay optional medical expenses until the beginning of the next year to get a head start on next year's deductible.

    Last year, I had some significant medical expenses, although, fortunately, they were for nothing too major. Toward the end of the year, I had met my individual deductible. When making my follow-up appointment, the doctor offered me appointments before the end of the year or in the following year. This was an easy choice; I took the appointment before the end of the year so all I had to pay was the small coinsurance amount. If I had waited until the following year, the deductible requirement would have started over, and I would have had to pay the entire cost of the visit myself.

8. Shop around to find medical providers with lower costs.

    Historically, consumers did not worry much about medical prices because their cost was approximately the same no matter how many medical services were used. But with high deductible plans, price is important because *you* are going to pay until your deductible is satisfied. If you're going to a specialist or for a medical procedure, ask your doctor to recommend several providers, as prices vary dramatically, and it will pay to shop around.

There are online price tools, and most insurance companies have their own online cost estimators, but they can be unreliable.[25] The best strategy is to call potential providers and ask for the standard price for the visit and the amount they expect to be reimbursed under your insurance plan, assuming the examination or procedure is covered. If they won't tell you, then try somewhere else or call your insurance company to find out the cost. Hopefully, the online options will improve in the near future to make shopping around much easier.

9. Review and keep all of the explanation-of-benefits (EOB) forms sent to you by your health insurance company.

Although you may be tempted to toss the EOB forms into your junk-mail pile, these forms are important, especially if you have a high deductible plan or a claim is denied. The EOB will show the date of service, the person in your family who was treated, and charges submitted by the medical provider to the insurance company. It will also show the insurance company's "allowable" charge, which is the maximum amount it will pay. In some plans, the provider can bill you for the difference between these amounts, even if the insurance covers the entire allowable charge. The EOB will also show the deductible requirement, co-insurance, and how much the insurance company paid to the provider if the claim was approved. It is a good place to see exactly how your health insurance works.

It's possible for EOBs to contain inaccuracies or mistakes, so review them thoroughly. If any claims were denied, the reasons

---

25 Elana Gordon, "Patients Want to Price-Shop for Care, But On-Line Tools Unreliable," NPR.org (Morning Edition), broadcast on November 30, 2015, http://www.npr.org/sections/health-shots/2015/11/30/453087857/patients-want-to-price-shop-for-care-but-online-tools-unreliable.

for the denial will be listed (although you may need to sort through the footnotes to find it). The EOB will also show any remaining deductible amount you need to satisfy for the year and the total amount the provider is allowed to bill you.

I don't recommend paying a bill from a provider until you receive the EOB form. At that point, you know how much the insurance company will pay and how much you are responsible for paying. Some providers bill you directly for the full amount as if there is no insurance, and then later provide a credit if they receive payment from the insurance company. That is in their best interest, but not yours. I don't want to pay my provider more than I need to, so I wait until I get the EOB to see what I am responsible for paying. Plus, waiting allows me to potentially negotiate a lower price for the medical service—see point number ten below. If you don't understand something on your EOB (don't feel stupid, they aren't easy to understand), call your insurance company for an explanation.

10. Negotiate prices down from the standard price to the allowable charge

    Doctors often have a standard price, which is higher than the negotiated amount they will accept from the insurance company (often called the "allowable charge"). However, it is common practice for the doctor to bill the standard price, even when patients have high deductible plans and are paying for the cost themselves.

    After you have shopped around and decide on which provider to use, call the doctor's office and explain that you have a high deductible plan and will be paying for their services through your deductible. Ask if you can pay the lower allowable charge, even if the office is allowed to charge you the standard charge. This is often an effective way of negotiating with your medical provider, as the logic is pretty hard to deny: "You would accept this from the insurance company, so will you accept it from me?" I have tried this several times and been successful most of the time in getting the charge reduced. However, it does not always work. Of course, you can try another provider to see if it will charge you less. Doing this *before* your treatment is more effective, but I have had success even after the treatment has been performed.

It is important to have health insurance. Health problems are a leading cause of individual bankruptcy and it doesn't take much for costs to pile up. Health insurance provisions can be confusing, so make sure you understand all the terms and requirements when you sign up for a plan. The health insurance company will follow the rules to the letter, and, if you don't go to the right provider or get a referral when it is needed, the insurance company may not pay.

High deductible plans are becoming more common. These plans require the patient to pay for all expenses until the deductible is satisfied. At that point, the insurance company starts to pay a percentage of the charges up to the maximum out-of-pocket cost. All these provisions mean the total cost of health care is much more than the monthly premium. An HSA is a great way to save to pay for the deductible requirement, as it has significant tax breaks.

There are ways to lower the cost of your health care. Shop around before seeing a doctor or getting a medical test to find the best prices in your area. If you are paying for the cost yourself, don't be afraid to ask to be charged the same price the doctor will accept from the insurance company. It makes so much sense; hopefully it will save you many cents too.

CHAPTER 11

How to Become Wealthy Using Annuities and Life Insurance

I WAS RECENTLY FLYING ON a Southwest Airlines flight out of Philadelphia to Los Angeles. As the 747 left the gate and we were taxiing toward the runway, the flight attendant announced that a wallet filled with money had been found, and asked if anyone wanted to claim it. He then said, "Now that I have your attention," and started into the preflight safety speech. I laughed to myself as I was now listening to the safety speech I have heard many times before. Why am I bringing up a clever flight attendant? Because I'm hoping the title of this chapter also got your attention, and, in a similar fashion, I'm going to provide you with information that you need to know. In this case, I'll explain what you need to know about using annuity and life insurance products as investments.

It seems to me that most of the advertising about annuities and life insurance as investments appeal to people's greed and focus on getting rich quick. All you have to do is buy their annuity or life insurance product, and you'll become incredibly wealthy. "Trust me," they say. "Come to my seminar, and I will teach you the secret way to become rich!"—and they will give you a free dinner in the process. They make it seem so easy, but is it true? I'll get to the bottom line right now: the answer is no. No annuity or insurance product is guaranteed to give you outrageous investment returns and make you wealthy.

The best way to become wealthy is to start saving as early as possible and save as much as you can. Take those savings, and invest responsibly in a range of investments to diversify your portfolio. How boring; I know, but it's the truth. An annuity and life insurance policy cannot fix the problem of having saved too little over the course of your life. No matter what you hear from some smooth salesperson, these products will not make you wealthy. That being said, annuities and life insurance do have some significant benefits and can be good products to buy in some circumstances. But they also have some significant downsides. In this chapter, you will learn about *both*.

Let's start with annuities. According to the *Merriam-Webster Dictionary*,[26] an annuity is a sum of money payable yearly or at other regular intervals. That definition describes the type of an annuity provided by the state lottery and an annuity sold by insurance companies called an immediate annuity or income annuity. An income annuity is not the annuity you see advertised on TV and pushed at those wealth seminars. That is a deferred annuity. However, income annuities are useful products when someone is near or in retirement. They are the main focus of chapter twelve, "The Secret Way to Never Outlive Your Money in Retirement."

A deferred annuity is the type of annuity sold to accumulate money for retirement. It's called a deferred annuity because the income payments do not begin immediately but, rather, are delayed (or deferred) until they are "elected" at a later date. Most people who own a deferred annuity policy never elect to start the income payments and simply use the deferred annuity to accumulate money for retirement.[27]

A common misconception is that a deferred annuity is an investment product. The truth is that it is an insurance product because it can only be purchased from an insurance company. You cannot purchase a deferred annuity from an investment company. My goal is to show you how to win at insurance, and I'm going to include how to win with an annuity as well. Our normal definition for winning at insurance is to be protected against financial ruin at the lowest cost possible. But the

---

26 *Merriam-Webster Online*, s.v. "annuity," accessed December 27, 2016, http://www.merriam-webster.com/dictionary/annuity.

27 Annuities are often called "contracts," but to be consistent with prior chapters, I will continue to call an annuity a "policy" or "product" in this chapter.

goal of purchasing a deferred annuity is not protecting against financial ruin; it is accumulating money for retirement. Therefore, we must expand our winning-at-insurance definition to include gaining some valuable feature that cannot be obtained for less cost elsewhere. That is how we win when considering an insurance product (a deferred annuity or life insurance) as an investment. We will evaluate the two features that attract many to purchase a deferred annuity: its investment guarantees and the deferral of tax on investment earnings.

Before we get into the details about those two items, let's start with how a deferred annuity works. It works in a similar way to a savings account at a bank. The purchaser of the deferred annuity gives the insurance company a check for the amount of the first deposit.[28] Although some deferred annuities permit additional deposits, it's common for only one deposit to be made into the policy (the single deposit is often called "a lump sum"). The first deposit makes up the annuity's **account value**, which is another name for the amount of money in the policy. Over time, the account value increases with interest credited and decreases when the company charges fees and expenses.

The simplest deferred annuity is a type called **a single premium deferred annuity** (SPDA). There are similar products called a fixed deferred annuity, **flexible premium deferred annuity** (FPDA), and multiyear guaranteed annuity. They have pretty much the same features and terms as an SPDA, so I'll focus on the SPDA. An SPDA has a stated initial interest rate that is guaranteed for a number of years; after the interest rate guarantee expires, future "renewal" interest rates are determined by the insurance company. The renewal interest rate cannot be less than the minimum interest rate that is guaranteed in the policy. The minimum guarantee is a nice feature (particularly in low interest rate environments) and offers some protection that the insurance company will provide a market rate of interest in the future.

---

28 Although the deposit into an annuity policy is often called the "premium," I will call it a deposit so it is not confused with the premium amount paid on an insurance policy.

To illustrate how an SPDA works, let's assume Jane is fifty years old and has $100,000 she wants to invest for retirement. She wants to grow that money as much as possible before retirement and is considering purchasing an SPDA. Her insurance agent is more than happy to provide her with various SPDA products to consider. Jane chooses an SPDA with a 3 percent interest rate that is guaranteed for five years. The SPDA's account starts with a value of $100,000 and, at the end of the five-year period, she will have $115,927 in her account.[29]

There are often many options to choose from with different guarantee periods and guaranteed interest rates, but every SPDA has the same basic calculations. Usually the guaranteed interest rate that is offered will be similar to what you would earn on a certificate of deposit at a bank. To make the deferred annuities more attractive to purchase, insurance companies add benefits like a **bonus payment** to the account value at the time of the first deposit, increasing the initial balance by an amount such as 1 or 2 percent. Another common bonus is a **bonus interest rate**, which is an above-market interest rate for a short period of time. These bonus payments look like free money, but, of course, they are not free.

No matter how amazing that initial guaranteed interest rate, bonus payments, and bonus interest looks, the amount of interest you will earn over the lifetime of an SPDA will be similar to what you can earn at a bank. Why? *Because insurance companies don't want you to know that they invest the money you give them to purchase the SPDA conservatively, just like a bank does.* Insurance companies take the money and invest it conservatively in highly rated, low-risk bonds. Highly rated bonds are safe investments but provide a lower return on average than more volatile investments like stocks.

Insurance companies must use the relatively low return they earn on their investments to pay for all their expenses (e.g., the commission paid to that insurance agent and those bonuses paid to you) and make their

---

[29] The account value at the end of five years equals the initial deposit increased by 3 percent interest compounded annually for five years. $100,000 \times (1.03)^5 = \$115,927$.

profit. The combination of conservative investing and large expenses means that over the long run, the interest rate paid on an SPDA will not be much better than what you could get if you purchased a run-of-the-mill certificate of deposit at a bank.

A big selling point of an SPDA is that it has favorable tax treatment. Most investments (including that bank certificate of deposit) require taxes to be paid on interest earned every year, but, with all insurance products, including deferred annuities, the owner pays no income tax on interest income earned each year. But that doesn't mean you never have to pay tax; the interest income is taxed when money is withdrawn. This is a valuable benefit. To understand the benefit of tax deferral, let's see how much in taxes Jane will save by purchasing the SPDA instead of putting the money into the bank where interest earnings are taxed each year.

To see the benefit of the tax deferral only, I need to keep the interest rate earned on the two products the same. Of course, they might not be the same in real life, which would also need to be taken into account when evaluating the benefit of the SPDA. I will then compare the value of the SPDA to the amount in the bank where both values are adjusted for taxes. Taxes are paid when we assume the money is withdrawn from the insurance company and will be paid each year on the money in the bank. I am going to assume only federal taxes are paid at a rate of 20 percent on the investment earnings.[30] (Note that the benefit of the tax deferral would be higher for those in a higher income tax bracket than 20 percent.)

As we discussed above, Jane deposits $100,000 into the SPDA and earns 3 percent for five years. At the end of the five-year period, she will have $115,927 in her SPDA account. Assuming Jane withdraws the money at the end of the five-year period, she must pay taxes on the interest earned and would have $112,742 left (80 percent of the interest

---

30 The calculation ignores the impact of state and other taxes. Since state taxes vary widely, I felt it would be better to show the impact of federal taxes only. People in states with high tax rates that apply to investment income would save more than what is shown in this illustration.

earned of $15,927 plus the original $100,000 deposit).[31] If Jane instead put her money into a bank account earning 3 percent interest she would have $112,590.[32] The tax deferral benefit in this example is the relatively modest amount of $152.

The small amount of benefit is due to the low interest rate and the time period of only five years. If this example were continued for twenty years (assuming the 3 percent interest rate was earned the entire time), the benefit of tax deferral would be $3,795. Also, the benefit of the tax deferral would be much larger if Jane earned a higher rate of interest. In this same example, if Jane could earn 5 percent for twenty years and paid 20 percent in taxes each year, she would have $13,589 more after taxes are taken into account from purchasing the SPDA than just putting the money in the bank.

The lesson learned from the numbers shown above is that the tax deferral benefit can be significant, but it depends on the circumstances. It has significantly less value in a low interest rate environment and if the purchaser needs the money relatively soon. The value also depends on the overall tax rate paid, including both federal and state tax rates. If a person does not pay much in taxes (if Jane were in a low federal tax bracket and in a low- or no-tax state), the tax deferral benefit would be small, even if interest rates were high and the time period were long.

The interest rate guarantee is nice, and the tax deferral benefit can be significant, but there some pretty big downsides to a deferred annuity like an SPDA. Once Jane purchases it, she can't easily get her money back for many years. The insurance company makes it expensive to leave by charging a penalty if she wants to take her money out of the policy. This penalty is called a surrender charge. The surrender charge can be

---

31 This calculation assumes no surrender charge and that the owner of the SPDA is older than fifty-nine-and-a-half years of age, so there is no early withdrawal penalty. Both surrender charges and early withdrawal penalties are discussed later in this chapter.

32 The value shown is computed assuming the initial deposit is at the beginning of the year and all taxes are paid from the bank account at the end of the year. Yearly taxes paid equal the amount of interest earned in each year multiplied by the assumed tax rate of 20 percent.

as high as 5 to 10 percent of the money withdrawn, although it typically decreases at the end of each year and ultimately is eliminated after a certain number of years (usually five to seven years after the purchase date).

Some SPDAs have another feature that works like a surrender charge called a **market value adjustment** (MVA). The MVA is applied when the owner of the SPDA wants to take money out of the policy prior to the end of the guaranteed interest rate period. The strange thing about the MVA is that, in some cases, it subtracts from the amount received (like a true surrender charge), and, in some cases, it adds to the amount received (almost like extra interest).

The MVA uses a relatively complex formula,[33] which protects the insurance company against changes in interest rates. The formula uses the number of years remaining on the interest rate guarantee and how interest rates have changed since purchase. As discussed above, insurance companies take the money provided by the SPDA customer and invest it in bonds so that they can pay the interest on the SPDA. When interest rates increase after the SPDA has been purchased, the value of the bonds purchased by the insurance company decreases. If the insurance company had to sell the bonds, it would incur a loss, so it protects itself by decreasing the amount it pays out by the amount of the MVA charge.

If interest rates decrease, then the value of the bonds purchased by the insurance company will increase in value. In this case, some SPDA policies will have an MVA that increases the amount received by the owners if they decide to surrender the policy prior to the end of the guaranteed interest rate period. However, it is important to note that not every SPDA policy will have an MVA that increases the value provided.[34] Some SPDAs will have a MVA that can only be a charge, and the MVA simply won't apply if interest rates decrease.

---

33 The MVA formula must be disclosed in the sales documents provided by the insurance company at the time of purchase. It is important to understand how a MVA works prior to purchasing the SPDA with one.

34 A "two-way" MVA can either be a charge or a credit, depending on how interest rates move. A "one-way" MVA only can be a charge or not apply. It is important to know how the MVA works prior to purchasing the SPDA.

Why does the insurance company make it so hard for Jane to get her money back? Like many things in life, it comes down to money. *Insurance companies don't want you to know that they initially lose money when they sell an SPDA or any deferred annuity, and they need you to keep the policy active for several years before they make a profit.* In the SPDA Jane purchased, the insurance company immediately loses money because it pays a commission to the insurance agent of 2 to 4 percent of the amount deposited into the account. The company has to earn enough to make up this loss before it can earn any profit. Therefore, the insurance company must make sure Jane keeps the policy for many years or charge her enough in the form of a surrender charge if she leaves too soon to make back any losses it incurs.

Another potential catch with all deferred annuities is a federal income tax penalty charged in certain circumstances when the money is taken out of the policy prior to retirement. The federal government wants a deferred annuity to be used to save for retirement and not simply as a way to dodge paying taxes. Therefore, the government requires that the money put into these products stays in the products until you get near retirement age (at least age fifty-nine-and-a-half years of age). To make sure this happens, the IRS charges a 10 percent tax penalty (on all interest earned on top of the income tax owed) if the money is taken out prior to the age of fifty-nine and a half.[35] The tax penalty is not charged if the money is immediately moved into another deferred annuity or is immediately used to purchase an income annuity. Taxation of deferred annuities can be complex. Please talk with a tax advisor for more information.

Before purchasing a deferred annuity, you should consider other products with the same deferred tax benefit. Employer-based retirement savings plans, like 401(k) and 403(b) plans, and individual retirement accounts (IRAs) have the same deferred tax benefits but with lower costs and fewer restrictions. Some 401(k) and 403(b) plans and some

---

35 Publication 575—Pension and Annuity Income, Internal Revenue Service, January 5, 2016, pages 33–36, https://www.irs.gov/pub/irs-pdf/p575.pdf.

IRAs have an additional benefit where "pretax money" (money that has never been federally taxed) can be deposited into the plan. Depositing pretax money "supercharges" the tax deferral benefit because you earn interest on the entire pretax amount instead of on the smaller amount you'd have left if income taxes were taken out first. Also, in some retirement plans, your employer will match a certain percentage of the money you put into the plan (e.g., a 50 percent match on the first 6 percent contributed). Each of these items makes these products better than a deferred annuity.

A quick sidenote on using pretax money to buy an annuity. It is possible to purchase a deferred annuity using pretax money. The insurance term is purchasing an annuity with "qualified money" or purchasing a **qualified annuity**. It is almost always a bad idea to purchase an annuity using pretax or qualified money. Qualified money is already tax deferred, so the tax-deferred status of the annuity has no additional value—losing one of the main benefits of the annuity in the first place. Only *very sophisticated investors* who *completely understand deferred annuities* should ever consider using qualified money to purchase a deferred annuity.

Always deposit as much as you can into employer-based or self-directed retirement plans before considering a deferred annuity. This is where your retirement savings should go first. The benefit of pretax money and an employer match are huge. They are not marketing gimmicks like the bonus payment or bonus interest offered with some deferred annuities. In particular, an employer match is a real additional return. It is essentially your employer paying you to save for retirement. An employer match cannot be equaled by anything offered in a deferred annuity or life insurance product.

However, the IRS limits the amount that you can put into tax-advantaged retirement plans each year, but deposits into deferred annuities have no limit. Therefore, if you have already put as much as you can into an employer-based retirement plan or an individually directed IRA, then a deferred annuity might be something to consider as part of your overall retirement portfolio. When purchasing a deferred annuity, remember to only use money that you will not need for a number of years, as it can be expensive to get your money back if you need it before retirement.

I have been focusing on the SPDA because it is a relatively simple product, which makes it easier to understand the mechanics of a deferred annuity. There are other types of deferred annuities called **fixed-indexed annuities** (also called **equity-indexed annuities** or **indexed annuities**) and variable annuities. Although they differ in some regards, the basic mechanics for all types are the same, with the main difference being how interest is credited to the account. Fixed-indexed and variable annuities are complicated products that should only be considered by sophisticated investors. They are loaded with fees and expenses that are difficult for the average person to see.

A fixed-indexed annuity is often marketed as an investment that will provide stock returns with a no-loss guarantee. But this description is not accurate. The owner receives interest based on how a chosen stock market index does—not real stock returns. The insurance company uses a complicated formula to determine the amount of the market returns that are credited to the account. The formula has limits and other adjustments that decreases the amount earned, compared to actually investing in the stock market. Importantly, the return earned is based only on the stock price change excluding the significant impact of dividends paid. And the guarantee is only that the value will never decrease (in other words a minimum of a 0 percent return). There is no guarantee of a positive return. For that, purchasers are locked into the policy for many years through large surrender charges and restrictions from getting their money back.

A variable annuity has some significant advantages (full disclosure: I own a variable annuity myself), but they are not appropriate for many people. A variable annuity policy invests directly in mutual funds, and the policy's value goes up and down based on how those mutual funds perform. There are loads and loads of charges and fees. The value of a variable annuity lies with the investment guarantees that can be purchased through optional policy terms called riders. Back in chapter five,

"Avoid These Common Mistakes," I discuss how life insurance riders are almost always bad deals, but this is not the case with variable annuity riders. You need to purchase a rider to get any value from a variable annuity.

I don't recommend a fixed-indexed annuity to anyone and would only suggest a variable annuity to sophisticated investors who are comfortable with investing in mutual funds and wading through the many terms and conditions contained in a variable annuity policy. Most people would do better by putting their retirement savings in a balanced portfolio of stocks and bonds, using low-cost mutual funds from a company such as the Vanguard Group® than purchasing a fixed-indexed or variable annuity. Yes, that strategy loses the tax deferral benefit but makes up for it with more investment options, low fees, and no surrender charges.

Before I move on to life insurance, I want alert you to an aggressive marketing campaign where "retirement specialists" purport that there is a "secret way" to invest your retirement savings in the stock market but still have it protected against a stock market crash. They won't tell you in advance, but many of these people are simply selling fixed-indexed annuities, often under the guise of providing independent retirement planning advice. I have been to presentations like this and listened to pitches on the radio; they can be convincing. But please don't do it! These so called "retirement specialists" are not independent advisors—they are simply slick insurance salespeople.

Fixed-indexed annuities are popular with insurance agents (and these hucksters) because insurance companies pay large commission percentages to the agents for selling them. The combination of the high commission percentage and customers depositing their lifetime retirement savings can lead to huge commission checks for agents. It greatly concerns me that these salespeople are simply looking for a "big score" by recommending a fixed-indexed annuity in circumstances where it is not appropriate. *Always* get an *independent* second opinion before buying any retirement annuity product. Once you have purchased one of these products, it is expensive to get your money back if you find out later it wasn't a great deal. It is critical that you understand exactly what you are buying and confirm that it is appropriate for your circumstances *before buying it*.

Certain types of cash-value life insurance products are also touted as ways to accumulate money. These products have names like fixed universal life, equity-indexed universal life, variable universal life, and whole life insurance. Like a deferred annuity, these life insurance products have the benefit of deferral of taxation on interest earned in the policy. The marketing pitch often goes like this: "Buy one of our great life insurance products, give us a good deal of money, we'll provide a competitive rate of interest or access to stock investments, and then you just sit back and watch your account value grow. You can use the money in the policy to save for a house or for retirement. And, you don't even have to pay taxes until you take the money out, and (enter somber voice) if you should unfortunately die, your generous death benefit will go to your heirs on a tax-free basis!" Sounds attractive, right? Unfortunately, it's only part of the story.

The first problem is that even if the life insurance policy is designed to be an investment, it is still life insurance. And you have to pay for the life insurance coverage, which will significantly decrease your overall return on the policy. If you don't need the life insurance, then it doesn't make any sense to pay for it. Investing responsibly or purchasing a deferred annuity is a much better choice than using life insurance as an investment. Of course, deferred annuities have significant problems, such as high expenses and fees, but they are better than life insurance to accumulate money if you don't need the life insurance.

If you do need life insurance, is it a good deal to buy a cash-value life insurance policy and use it as a savings tool as well? Generally, the answer is no. I prefer to purchase term insurance if I need life insurance and save for retirement using low cost mutual funds or deferred annuity products with excellent guarantees. The biggest problem with using cash-value life insurance is that you cannot use the policy as both life insurance and a savings vehicle at the same time.

If you need the money from the policy while you are alive, you have three options.

Option one: You can completely cancel or surrender the policy, thus losing the life insurance protection. Also, you may have to pay an expensive surrender charge unless you purchased the policy a long time ago.

Option two: If your policy allows it, you could take out some of the money in the policy and keep the policy in force. Many life insurance policies will allow you to surrender a small amount of the account value without any surrender charge being applied. But this may not be enough money to meet your needs. Also, you may still lose your insurance protection unless you put more money into the policy in the future.

Option three: You could take a **policy loan** from the policy. With a policy loan, you essentially borrow your own money and pay yourself interest within the life insurance policy. It still costs you money of course, because the insurance company still takes a piece of the action. Policy loans can be useful, but taking too large a policy loan can lead to the policy running out of money and leaving you without the life insurance protection you need.

The bottom line is that gaining access to the money within a cash-value life insurance policy without canceling the entire policy is not simple and may be expensive. I don't recommend purchasing cash-value life insurance other than in certain estate tax situations for wealthy individuals. If that applies to you, then congratulations on your success! Just make sure you get good independent advice before plunking down your family fortune for one of these policies.

The final issue with using life insurance as a savings vehicle is transparency. I'm sure you'll agree with me that no insurance policy is easy to understand. That being said, an SPDA is relatively straightforward, as the balance grows with interest each year. Yes, there could be a surrender charge and some other fees, but that's about it. Life insurance has many more moving parts. Yes, there is a credited interest rate (sometimes called a dividend interest rate), but there is also the cost of insurance and other fees and expenses which can be very hard to identify. As

I discussed in chapter five, "Avoid These Common Mistakes," shopping around for insurance is important to getting the best price, but the more features and complexities in a product makes it hard to understand if you are getting a good deal. I have been asked to compare cash-value life insurance policies for friends and it's almost impossible to do. Make sure you understand exactly what you're signing up for before putting your name on the dotted line.

You won't become wealthy simply by purchasing a product from a life insurance company. That being said, there are some benefits that you should know about. An SPDA is a way to save money for retirement that has the benefit of tax deferral on interest earned, but, in general, an SPDA will have low returns. Fixed-indexed annuities are much more complicated than they seem, and I find it hard to recommend them to anyone. Variable annuities can be good products but they are complex and should only be purchased by sophisticated investors who completely understand and accept the high fees and expenses buried within the policy. When considering a deferred annuity, focus on the guarantees, and evaluate whether the guarantees are good enough to make the downsides (lack of access to the funds, high expenses and fees, surrender charges) worth it.

A life insurance policy can be used as a savings vehicle, but it's not easy to get your money back if you need it. Also, it makes no sense to pay for life insurance if you actually don't need it. Cash-value life insurance policies like traditional life, universal life, variable life, and indexed universal life are complicated products with a number of moving pieces. It is almost impossible to comparison shop among different company's products. I prefer purchasing term insurance if I need life insurance and investing with an investment company or a deferred annuity. Remember, if you find an annuity or life insurance product you think will be a good investment, always get an independent second opinion before buying.

CHAPTER 12

THE SECRET WAY TO NEVER OUTLIVE YOUR MONEY IN RETIREMENT

AS PEOPLE REACH RETIREMENT AGE, the concern about possibly outliving their money is common. Saving as much as possible for retirement is a concept most people understand. But how to best spend your savings during retirement is a big mystery. My seventy-three-year old father recently sought my advice about his financial future. After working many years as an orthodontist in a job he loves, he started to cut back his hours, as he transitioned toward retirement.

Although he had done a great job saving, his instinct was to start restricting his spending now that he was not bringing in as much in salary. "I need to spend less, so my retirement savings won't decrease," he told me. As we talked, I learned his biggest fear was running out of money during retirement. Of course, he will need to spend some of his retirement savings, but how much should he spend when he doesn't know how long he will be in retirement? How does he guarantee he will never run out of money? It seemed to him like an impossible problem to solve.

In my experience, this question is often answered in a way that "probably will work" because there are many unknowns. We don't know how long we will be in retirement. We don't know how much we will earn in the future on our investments. We don't know how much savings is really enough. Due to these uncertainties, some retirement experts will create a complicated model to predict how much a retiree can spend to be 90 or 95 percent sure that they will never run out of money. Or they will explain a simple "rule of thumb" that works *most of the time*. They could come up with a 100 percent certain solution, but it will require being fabulously rich before you can retire. *This is not good enough.* I am going to show you a fail-safe way to determine how much you need to never outlive your money. Not probably or likely, but 100 percent certain, with no tricks, conditions, or limitations. After all, we all only get one retirement, and there are no "do-overs" if things don't work out.

Before I go any further, let me add one important dose of reality about those last statements. The strategy I will explain will not address the problem of having too little money saved for retirement to start with. How much you will need will depend on when you retire and how much in income you believe you need during retirement. If you only have a small amount of money saved for retirement, working longer to accumulate more savings or spending less in retirement will be necessary. As many of us will live a long time in retirement, substantial savings will be required. But the one thing I can assure you is that my strategy doesn't require being independently wealthy to work.

To see how much is needed to make it through retirement, let me introduce you to Charlie. Charlie is sixty-five and is thinking about retiring. He wants to figure out how much he needs to have saved so he never outlives his money. Charlie is in good health for his age and hopes to have a long retirement. To simplify the analysis, I will assume that Charlie is not married and has money saved in the bank that he wants to use to fund his retirement. In other words, the money being used will not be taxed when it is taken from the bank.[36] For simplicity's sake, I will do all of the calculations on a pretax basis.

Rules relating to taxation of social security payments and money in pension plans are complex. Some retirement savings can be accessed without paying any tax (e.g., a Roth IRA), and money taken from other retirement savings accounts are taxed at regular income tax rates (e.g., 401(k) plans

---

36 Money in many tax-deferred retirement accounts will be taxed when withdrawn from the accounts. Therefore, a retiree will need more money than is shown in the example if the money is coming from a tax-deferred account. Since tax rates vary based on individual circumstances, I felt it would be too complex to use money in retirement accounts in this analysis.

and ordinary Individual Retirement Accounts). There are penalties for using retirement money at too young an age and also for keeping money too long in a retirement account.[37] The tax penalties can be severe. A person's tax situation will influence what money to use first from your retirement accounts. I strongly recommend consulting a tax professional when planning for retirement, as taxes will have a significant impact on the best way to generate income during retirement.

The first thing Charlie needs to do is to figure out how much annual or monthly income he needs to live comfortably in retirement. The number is likely less than what he was making before retirement, since some of his salary was going to fund his retirement and increase his savings. At this point in his life, he needs to determine if he has enough saved to be OK during retirement. As I mentioned in chapter six ("How Much Life Insurance Do I Need?"), a certified financial planner can be helpful in understanding your financial situation.

Let's assume Charlie hired a certified financial planner who, after reviewing Charlie's current spending, determined if he retired now, he would need a total of $5,000 per month ($60,000 per year) in pre-tax income to pay his expenses. If Charlie currently needs $5,000 per month in income, then he will need more in the future due to inflation. Every year the things we buy increase in price. Over the last fifteen years, inflation in the United States, as measured by the Consumer Price Index (CPI), has averaged about 2 percent per year.[38] It has been higher in some time periods and lower in others. Since Charlie is planning for his entire future lifetime, the income he needs must increase by at least the amount of inflation so that he will maintain the same purchasing power.

---

[37] There are significant penalties for keeping money in tax-deferred retirement accounts for too long. Tax penalties apply if required mandatory distributions from retirement accounts do not start prior to age 70½. See a tax professional for more information.

[38] "Consumer Price Index for All Urban Consumers: All Items," Federal Reserve Bank of St. Louis, Economic Research Division, accessed October 29, 2016, https://fred.stlouisfed.org/series/CPIAUCSL. January 1, 2016 CPI of 238.107 compared to January 1, 2001 CPI of 175.600 on an annual basis.

In the illustrative example below, we will assume a future inflation rate of 2 percent each year.[39]

Charlie reviewed all his assets and retirement accounts with the financial planner. He has a **defined-benefit retirement plan** from his employer that will pay him $1,000 per month for life, and the financial planner helped him find out that he's entitled to Social Security of $1,500 per month ($18,000 per year) for life. Therefore, Charlie needs an additional $2,500 of income per month today ($2,500 plus the defined-benefit plan income of $1,000 plus Social Security of $1,500 equals $5,000) to meet his targeted income. Social security payments are indexed with inflation, and, for simplicity, I'll assume Charlie's defined-benefit pension will also increase with inflation (although, in reality, many payments from defined-benefit plans remain level each year).

Before I reveal my recommended strategy, let's examine how some other common retirement strategies might work. A popular strategy is to have enough saved so one can live off the interest on retirement savings. The logic of this strategy is that if spending exactly equals the interest earned, then the overall amount of the retirement assets will stay the same and never decrease.

This strategy also often includes investing in relatively safe investments like bonds to be sure of getting a certain amount of interest each year. Let's assume that Charlie invests his assets conservatively and will earn a 4 percent return every year. Charlie's goal is to generate $2,500 per month ($30,000 per year) on a pretax basis with the income increasing each year by 2 percent to keep up with inflation. Therefore, Charlie would need $1,500,000 in retirement assets.[40] That is a lot of money!

---

39 The right inflation assumption to use is impossible to know in advance. Therefore, there is really no right answer other than some inflation should be assumed. I chose 2 percent but higher or lower assumptions would also be appropriate. In other words, never assume 0 percent inflation when performing retirement calculations.

40 The $1,500,000 value equals the $30,000 per year income requirement divided by the 4 percent income rate, less the 2 percent inflation rate. This is a geometrically increasing annuity whose present value is $30,000 divided by (0.04 − 0.02).

But there is an even bigger problem than that it requires a ridiculous amount of money. Charlie has to earn at least 4 percent interest *every year* on his savings for the strategy to work. But no one knows what interest rates will be in the future. A prolonged period of low interest rates would mean that Charlie would have to immediately decrease how much he could spend. Most people can't just decrease their spending, as they have regular expenses that must be paid. If Charlie doesn't earn 4 percent interest and cannot lower his spending, then he will have to use some of the retirement savings to meet his expenses. This lowers the amount left and also decreases the amount of interest earned in the following year. This vicious cycle can quickly lead to having no retirement savings left—a total disaster.

Some may say that the $1.5 million number is way too high because it assumes Charlie will live forever. It's a good point. The problem is that Charlie doesn't know exactly how long he will need the money. Another common strategy addresses this issue by choosing a conservative "target age," like ninety-five, for how long the money needs to last. If everything goes according to plan, then Charlie knows exactly how much he can spend each year, based on that budget.

Although this strategy sounds reasonable, I don't recommend it because spending your retirement savings with the expectation of living to some target age (no matter what age is picked) is a "lose-lose" situation. To understand why, let's first see how much money Charlie would need to retire using this strategy. As discussed above, Charlie needs $2,500 a month in income at retirement. The income needs to increase with inflation at 2 percent and we are going to assume he can earn 4 percent on his savings forever.[41] All calculations are before considering taxes (in other words, they are "pretax"). Using the target age of ninety-five, Charlie needs to make his money last for thirty years, as he is currently sixty-five. Doing some math, this means that Charlie needs about

---

41 The 2 percent increase in income will happen at the end of each year. Charlie will receive $2,500 in monthly income for all of the first year, then $2,550 = $2,500 × 1.02 in the second year, and so on, with each year's income increasing by 2 percent.

The Secret Way to Never Outlive Your Money in Retirement

$670,000 before he can retire.[42] This too is a lot of money but is much less than the $1.5 million we computed in the previous method.

I see this methodology as a "lose-lose" because if the Charlie dies before the target age, he has underenjoyed his retirement. If Charlie only lives to eighty-five, he would have needed only about $490,000 to get the same monthly income (instead of the $670,000 needed to make it to age ninety-five).[43] He could have retired earlier or could have spent more during the twenty years of his retirement. He could have used the extra $180,000 to take that dream trip to Australia, gone to that baseball fantasy camp when he could still enjoy it, or bought that new car he wanted. This is a sad situation indeed, as most people don't have enough money to live as well as they would like to in retirement. But because Charlie doesn't know how long he will need the money, he has to be conservative and underspend in case he lives too long.

If Charlie lives a long time, the situation becomes his worst nightmare. With every passing year, the money in Charlie's retirement account gets smaller and smaller. At age eighty-five, he has about $400,000 left in his retirement savings. At age ninety, it is down to $230,000 and decreasing rapidly. He wants to enjoy the later years of his life, but his dwindling retirement savings account is a constant worry. All he can think about is that he might live past the target age of ninety-five and completely run out of money!

But at this stage in his life, even if he wanted to, it's too late to correct the situation. He won't be able to earn much money, as he is too old to even be a Walmart greeter. A few years later, at age ninety-five, his retirement savings are completely gone—which, of course, is by design. Having spent his entire savings, he would have to live on Social Security and his defined-benefit pension (less than he needs) or rely on

---

42 The calculation computed the present value of the monthly income required assuming the $2,500 was at the end of the first month. The present value was computed using monthly interest compounding. All values in this chapter are rounded to the nearest $10,000, with the exact value shown in the footnotes. In this case, the exact amount needed is $667,852.

43 The exact amount needed is $488,261.

the support of his family—the exact situation he so desperately wanted to avoid.

Of course, Charlie might not live past age ninety-five, but it is projected that living to one hundred will become more and more common in the near future.[44] And we want to be 100 percent sure that Charlie will not outlive his money. Of course, the calculation could be changed to be certain that he will never outlive his money by assuming a really old target age, like 115. But this is not a practical solution for most people, as it increases the amount needed to a whopping $930,000. Plus, assuming a superlong lifetime virtually guarantees significantly under-enjoying one's retirement. Or most likely, once Charlie sees he needs that much to retire, he'll keep punching that time clock for many more years, thinking he can't really afford to retire until he saves much more money—or ever.

It might appear impossible to guarantee that you will never outlive your retirement savings because there are so many unknowns and things out of your control. There is great uncertainty (we don't know how much interest we'll earn on our savings or how long we're going to be in retirement) that may lead to a large financial loss (having no retirement savings left), where a person could be financially ruined (needing money in retirement when there is no means to earn it). Does this problem sound familiar?

I hope it does, as this is exactly what we have been discussing in this book! Insurance policies are designed to deal with *uncertain situations* where something *outside of one's control* might lead to *financial ruin*. Insurance solves problems like these that people cannot solve on their own. The problem of how to not outlive your retirement savings is like protecting against an unexpected death or your house burning down. Insurance companies combine many people together so that they can

---

[44] Lynda Gratton and Andrew Scott, "How Work Will Change When Most of Us Live to 100," *Harvard Business Review,* June 27, 2016, https://hbr.org/2016/06/how-work-will-change-when-most-of-us-live-to-100.

afford to pay money to those few people who need the money to avoid financial ruin.

The insurance product that protects against outliving one's money in retirement is called a lifetime income annuity. A lifetime income annuity is similar to Charlie's traditional defined-benefit pension plan where he receives monthly income payments for life. By buying a lifetime income annuity, Charlie will transfer the risk of living too long to the insurance company. The insurance company will guarantee payments for Charlie's entire lifetime, no matter how long he lives.

Charlie went to his insurance agent and asked for a quote for a lifetime income annuity where the insurance company will guarantee payments for life. Before I get into the numbers, I need to explain a few things about why relatively few lifetime income annuities are sold. Most insurance agents hate selling a lifetime income annuity and will likely suggest you purchase something else. The cynical side of me believes that the dislike is due to the low commissions paid on income annuities and the higher commissions paid on "savings products" like deferred annuities and cash-value life insurance. In other words, insurance agents make much more money helping you save for retirement than helping you spend it.

Regardless of motive, let's walk through each of the common criticisms of a lifetime income annuity so that you get the full picture of how the product can protect against outliving one's money in retirement. Then you can make up your own mind for what is best for you. At the risk of being repetitive (my apologies if you find it so), I also want to remind you of the theme in this book: winning means purchasing insurance (a lifetime income annuity in this case) that protects against financial ruin at the lowest cost possible.

OK. Here are the *false* reasons you might hear in an attempt to convince you against purchasing a lifetime income annuity:

1. **The investment returns on an income annuity are terrible.**

    I hope this one is an easy one for you by now. The retiree is purchasing the lifetime income annuity as an insurance policy to never outlive his or her money at retirement, not as an investment. As I explained way back in chapter two, "How to Win at Insurance," trying to make money on an insurance policy is a mistake. Insurance is needed for those risks in life you cannot protect on your own. Outliving one's money in retirement is one of those risks.

2. **You don't want to lose control of most of your savings by giving it to the insurance company. You would be better off by just investing it yourself and keeping control.**

It is difficult to write a large check to the insurance company for a lifetime income annuity as you *are* losing control of that part of your savings. But as I explained above, the lifetime income annuity provides peace of mind that you will never outlive your money. Insurance companies are designed to play this role, and this is a risk you cannot protect against yourself, even if you invest wisely. As I will show below in point four, the cost of this protection can be gained at a much lower price than most people think.

3. **You should never purchase a lifetime income annuity without a guaranteed number of payments. If you die soon after purchasing the annuity, you will never get your money's worth from the policy.**

Most agents will suggest purchasing a lifetime income annuity with a certain number of guaranteed payments, called a **certain period**. This is a common mistake. All a certain period does is increase the amount ultimately paid by the insurance company, thereby increasing the price it has to charge for the policy. We want to get the insurance against outliving our money during retirement at the lowest cost possible. A lifetime income annuity with no certain period is the cheapest way to accomplish this goal.

That being said, *anyone with a serious, life-threatening illness, who is not in good overall health, or who has a relatively short life expectancy should never purchase a lifetime income annuity.* The goal here is to protect against living too long. If that is unlikely to happen, then insurance to protect against that risk is not needed.

4. **Income annuities are expensive.**

This one is true, but there is an easy solution. The most common type of lifetime income annuity is an **immediate lifetime income annuity,** which is expensive. In an immediate lifetime income annuity, the monthly income starts right after the policy is purchased, and the insurance company knows it will make many payments. But Charlie's risk is not that he won't be able to make ends meet next month or even over the next few years. It is having no money when he is very old. So the solution to the problem is to defer the start date of the income annuity payments until he really needs them.

The principle is similar to my friend Pete and his life insurance decision back in chapter six, "How Much Life Insurance Do I Need?" You might remember that Pete wanted life insurance to protect his daughter if he passed away prematurely. His insurance agent suggested coverage for thirty years, but I helped him understand that fifteen years of coverage was all he needed. The probability of his premature death over the next fifteen years was low, leading to a dramatically lower price.

Since Charlie really only needs the guaranteed income payments when he is much older, he can save a huge amount of money by having the payments start at a relatively old age, like at eighty-five. Since the insurance company will make many fewer payments, it charges a much lower price. This product is commonly called a **deferred lifetime income annuity.** A deferred lifetime income annuity also goes by the name of **longevity insurance.** A deferred lifetime income annuity is not the same as the deferred annuity we discussed in chapter eleven, "How to Become Wealthy Using Annuities and Life Insurance," as a deferred annuity is used to accumulate assets for retirement not provide income.

Let's see how this would work for Charlie. First, we'll start by considering an immediate lifetime income annuity for Charlie. Please note that all prices shown below are for illustrative purposes and are only representative of the cost of these options on the date the quotes were obtained from an online price-comparison website.[45] The lifetime income annuity paying $2,500 in monthly income, increasing by 2 percent per year, starting immediately, would cost approximately $570,000.[46]

Prices for lifetime income annuities change constantly, and the price in reality for the income shown may be higher or lower than what is shown in this example, depending on market conditions. The price of a lifetime income annuity for a woman will be higher, since women generally live longer than men. Many people are married and would want to consider a **joint-life lifetime income annuity** covering both spouses. This will cost more than a lifetime income annuity on only one person but will protect against either of the spouses outliving their retirement money.

The $570,000 is still a lot of money. However, it is less than it would take for Charlie to protect himself, assuming a target age of ninety-five (that value, from above, was $670,000). It does make sure Charlie never outlives his money but does have some serious downsides that I discussed above (loss of control of a large amount of your savings and it is expensive). It is an answer, but not the best one.

The best answer is for Charlie to purchase a deferred lifetime income annuity. It is the cheapest way to proceed because it protects against the risk of outliving one's money and nothing else. Insurance companies sold about $2.7 billion of deferred income annuities in 2015, according

---

45 All income annuity quotes were obtained from the immediateannuities.com aggregator website on December 30, 2016.
46 The median (middle) of the seven quotes provided was used to provide an illustration of what Charlie might have to pay to receive the income he requires. Quotes used were for a sixty-five-year-old male, residing in Pennsylvania. Value shown based on $500,000 quote with income pro-rated as necessary. Not all quotes are from the same company. All quotes should be used for illustrative purposes only. The exact amount is $571,037.

to the LIMRA Secure Retirement Institute.[47] The Institute "anticipate[s] DIA [deferred income annuity] sales to increase at a slow but steady pace for the foreseeable future."

A welcome development relating to deferred income annuities was when the IRS recently released a rule allowing for favorable tax treatment for these types of policies (the IRS calls a deferred income annuity a "Qualified Longevity Annuity Contract" or QLAC).[48] Under certain circumstances, the IRS will exclude money in a **defined-contribution retirement plans** like an IRA from mandatory required distributions (there are penalties if a person does not use the money in retirement accounts quickly enough) if the money is used to purchase a QLAC. The annuity contract must be purchased from an insurance company on or after July 2, 2014, with the income starting no later than age eighty-five. Restrictions and limitations apply.[49] Please consult a tax advisor prior to purchasing any deferred income annuity if you are interested in using it in this way.

The longer Charlie waits to receive income, the cheaper the price will be because the insurance company knows it will pay less on the policy. How long to defer the payments is an individual decision that needs to be based on how much money you have saved for retirement and the price difference among the deferral periods offered by the insurance company when one is shopping for one of these products. I will assume

---

47 "LIMRA Secure Retirement Institute: Indexed Annuities Break Quarterly and Annual Sales Records," limra.com, last modified February 23, 2016, http://www.limra.com/Posts/PR/News_Releases/LIMRA_Secure_Retirement_Institute__Indexed_Annuities_Break_Quarterly_and_Annual_Sales_Records.aspx. Only a relatively small portion of these deferred income annuity sales were for lifetime income only. Most sales would include a certain period as well, which, in my view, is a mistake.

48 "Publication 7004 (Rev. 4-2016) Catalog Number 36179Q," Department of the Treasury, Internal Revenue Service, accessed December 4, 2016, https://www.irs.gov/pub/irs-pdf/p7004.pdf. See page 4, Section V—"Qualified Longevity Annuity Contracts."

49 No more than $125,000 or 25 percent of one's retirement savings can be used to purchase the deferred income annuity, and the deferred payments must begin no later than age eighty-five. Please see a tax advisor before purchasing one of these policies.

that Charlie decides to have the deferred lifetime income begin at age eighty-five (in twenty years).

Assuming 2 percent inflation each year, Charlie would need the annuity to provide $3,715 per month to have the same purchasing power in twenty years that $2,500 per month has today.[50] Charlie shopped around and found the cost of the deferred lifetime income annuity starting at age eighty-five, with a monthly payment of $3,715 that will increase by 2 percent every year thereafter, was only about $110,000.[51]

This number seems impossibly small but remember the price charged by the insurance company is based on the amount it expects to pay in the future. Many people will not make it to age eighty-five. Those who do make it to age eighty-five would not be expected to receive many payments as only a few people will live into their nineties or make it to one-hundred years old. Of course, the people who die before receiving any or many payments did not need the money. To keep the price as low as possible, one must accept the possibility of not receiving any payments if they are not needed.

The beauty of this strategy is that for a one-time payment of $110,000, Charlie has total peace of mind that he *will never outlive his money during retirement*. After Charlie purchases the deferred lifetime income annuity, the major sources of his financial insecurity during retirement are gone. He only needs to plan for the next twenty years, knowing that the insurance company will pay him the guaranteed income for life thereafter.

He can then compute how much money he would need to save for retirement to make it over the next twenty years. Like determining the inflation assumption discussed above, there is no correct answer on how

---

[50] $\$2{,}500 \times (1.02)^{20} = \$3{,}714.87$

[51] The median (middle) of the seven quotes provided was used to provide an illustration of what Charlie might have to pay to receive lifetime income starting at age eighty-five. No payments are received if Charlie dies before age eighty-five. Quotes used were for a sixty-five-year-old male, residing in Pennsylvania. Value shown based on a $500,000 quote, with income pro-rated as necessary. Exact amount computed was $110,299. For illustrative purposes only.

to perform this calculation.[52] I am going to be consistent with the calculations above and assume Charlie will earn 4 percent in interest every year and require income payments that increase by 2 percent per year. An important thing to note here is that it is much more feasible to determine reasonable assumptions for a known future period of time, like the next twenty years, than over one's unknown future lifetime.

To fund his retirement for the next twenty years, Charlie would need an additional $490,000 in savings to make it until the annuity payments from the insurance company begin in twenty years.[53] In total, Charlie would need about $600,000 of retirement savings, including the cost of the deferred lifetime income annuity.[54] I know some of you are thinking that is a lot of money just to guarantee $2,500 of income per month ($30,000 per year) growing at 2 percent each year for life. That is understandable, as it is a lot of money. But let's put it into perspective. A sixty-five-year old has a future life expectancy of almost eighteen years, according to the Social Security Administration.[55] That means that half of all sixty-five-year old men will live to age eighty-three, with many of them living into their late eighties and nineties, and a few into their hundreds. If Charlie lives to age eighty-three, as half will do, he will have received a total of over $640,000 in income over the eighteen years.[56]

The beauty of the deferred lifetime income annuity is total peace of mind. If Charlie had $600,000 saved, he would be able to protect

---

52 It would be prudent to use a conservative interest earned rate in this calculation. Consult a financial advisor or insurance expert for assistance in determining the best assumption in your circumstances.
53 The calculation computed the present value of the monthly income required for 20 years with payments of $2,500 per month, increasing by 2 percent per year. The present value was computed using monthly interest compounding. Exact amount is $488,261.
54 This includes $110,000 for the deferred lifetime income annuity, plus $490,000 for the first twenty years of income.
55 "Life Actuarial Table—Period Life Table, 2013," Social Security Administration—Office of the Chief Actuary, accessed November 12, 2016, https://www.ssa.gov/oact/STATS/table4c6.html.
56 The $642,261 is the sum of all of the monthly income Charlie would receive, starting at age sixty-five until he turns eighty-three. The income begins at $2,500 per month and increases by 2 percent per year.

himself for what hopefully will be many, many years in retirement with a *100 percent guarantee* of never outliving his money. If he didn't have that much money, he would need to work longer or accept less income in the future. If after he purchases the annuity, but before the income starts in twenty years, something goes wrong, like he doesn't earn enough in interest or prices increase dramatically, Charlie is young enough to fix it by getting a part-time job or temporarily spending less. When Charlie is really old and at the most vulnerable point in his life, he can sleep soundly knowing that the monthly income he needs will arrive each and every month for the rest of his life, no matter how long he lives.

Everyone entering retirement should consider purchasing an income annuity with a lifetime guarantee unless the person has a serious illness or disease that is expected to significantly shorten his or her expected future lifetime or has so much money saved that outliving one's money is not a concern. The lifetime guarantee is a valuable benefit that you can only purchase from an insurance company and is the only way to be certain you will never outlive your money. I recommend working with an independent, certified financial planner to determine how much income you need during retirement and that you consider a deferred lifetime income annuity as part of a sound retirement plan.

The goal is to pass the risk of living too long and not earning enough interest on your savings onto the insurance company. Like your house burning down, it is not a risk that most people can personally protect against. A person has only one life. The idea is to *guarantee* that you have enough money, no matter how long your retirement lasts, and to enjoy your retirement years as much as possible. Yes, a retiree might do better by not buying the annuity and just investing the money instead…but he or she might also run out of money. Those who live a long time will receive so much more from the income annuity than what they could obtain by investing the money themselves. A deferred lifetime income annuity is the secret way to never outlive your money during retirement.

CHAPTER 13

An Insurance Action Plan

REVIEWING AND OPTIMIZING ALL YOUR insurance at once can be an overwhelming exercise. It can be hard to figure out where to start. In our final chapter, I present a step-by-step action plan to help address your insurance needs.

STEP 1: IDENTIFY YOUR LARGEST RISKS

What are the most important risks that you face right now? Review chapter three ("What Type of Insurance Do I Need?"), and make of list of each of the insurance products you need. Which risk has the largest possibility of ruining you financially? Focus on the biggest risks first.

Make sure to consider all types of insurance products, as you may have a risk that you're not aware of at this moment. Below, I list some typical needs for varying age groups. I'm not going to discuss car or homeowner's insurance, as those policies are usually required as part of purchasing the car or house. The guidelines below are general, so you should modify, as needed, for your situation.

Ages twenty to twenty-nine: Health insurance and disability insurance are must-haves for most people in this age group. If you rely on your income to survive, you need disability insurance, and the best time to buy it is when you are young. Some employers will offer disability insurance to their employees, but if your employer does not, you need an individual disability policy.

Ages thirty to thirty-nine: After a wedding or the birth/adoption of a child, consider your life insurance needs. If someone else will depend on your income in the future, then you need life insurance. Make sure your loved ones are protected.

Ages forty to forty-nine: Hopefully, by this age, you have health insurance, disability insurance, and some life insurance. Those in their forties should reevaluate whether they have enough life insurance. Life insurance purchased years ago many not be enough now, as you may have more people who rely on you financially. Make sure you have enough, as was discussed in chapter six ("How Much Life Insurance Do I Need?").

Also, during your forties, you may have saved some money for retirement. If you have put the maximum into employer-based or individual retirement accounts and still have money available that you are certain you will not need for many years, then you might consider an annuity. See chapter eleven, "How to Become Wealthy Using Annuities and Life Insurance," and make sure you get an independent second opinion before buying any annuity product.

Ages fifty to fifty-nine: This is the time to really focus on saving for a secure retirement, as a person's peak earning years are often between ages fifty and fifty-nine. This is also a reasonable time to consider long-term care insurance, but, as I discuss in chapter three ("What Type of Insurance Do I Need?"), it is not an insurance product I believe most people need.

Ages sixty and up: This is the time to start considering a deferred lifetime income annuity. Deferred lifetime income annuities with long deferral periods cost much less than those with shorter deferral periods. In other words, if you want lifetime income that starts at age eighty-five, purchasing a deferred lifetime income annuity at age sixty-five is significantly cheaper than purchasing it at age seventy-five. It is cheaper because the insurance company expects to make fewer payments if the payments start in twenty years versus in only ten. There is no right age to consider purchasing a deferred income annuity, but, as we discussed in chapter twelve ("The Secret Way to Never Outlive Your Money in Retirement"), it is a great addition to a retirement plan.

STEP 2: FIND A KNOWLEDGEABLE AND TRUSTED INSURANCE AGENT

After you have identified your largest risks, you will need to buy insurance protection. Some products, like term life insurance, can be purchased through the Internet, but buying insurance often means finding a good insurance agent to help you find the right product for your circumstances. I understand that this is easier said than done, but it is worth the effort, as having a good insurance agent can save you money and aggravation.

Getting a recommendation from a friend or coworker about a good agent is always a plus, but you can't totally rely on others' opinions. I have seen many instances where a person finds an agent from a friend's recommendation only to find that the agent is not as good as advertised. Make up your own mind if any agent is right for you. See chapter four ("Why Is That Insurance Agent So Friendly?") about what to look for in a good insurance agent.

The agent should fully understand the product being sold and be able to explain both the pros and the cons to you. That being said, *you* need to totally understand what you're buying as well. It is a good idea to read the policy language and understand it completely before buying. In some cases, it will be helpful to get a second, independent opinion to make sure the information the insurance agent is telling you is correct. A second opinion may not be necessary if the insurance is relatively simple, like term or car insurance, but a second opinion is critical if you are considering buying more complicated insurance products like long-term care or using life insurance or an annuity as an investment.

Here is a simple test to see if you have a good agent. After completing an assessment of your insurance needs, as I advised in step one, contact your insurance agent, and set up a meeting. Without saying what you found in step one, ask the agent to do his or her own assessment of your insurance needs. The agent should identify the same or similar risks as you did. If you have good insurance coverage, the agent should not try to sell you anything. If the agent immediately tries to sell you something that you know you don't need or starts trying to sell you a high-commission product like an annuity, be suspicious. If the agent pushes hard to make a sale, then you probably need to find a new agent.

STEP 3: SHOP AROUND FOR INSURANCE, MAKING SURE TO GET QUOTES FROM A NUMBER OF INSURANCE COMPANIES

One of the most common mistakes people make with insurance is not shopping around. An independent insurance agent should provide price quotes from a number of different insurance companies. If you don't shop around, you can't be sure you're getting the best price. It can be difficult to compare products, as some insurance companies add additional insurance (often called riders) to the policy to make it hard to compare. A good insurance agent will give you the price for the base coverage without any riders so that you can compare apples to apples.

STEP 4: REVIEW YOUR CAR AND HOMEOWNER'S DEDUCTIBLES

As we discussed in chapter nine ("How to Choose the Right Car and Homeowner's Insurance Deductible"), you might be able to save some money by changing the deductible on your car and homeowner's insurance. Many people have too small a deductible on these policies. Not only does this lead to possibly paying more in premiums each year, it gives you an incentive to make more claims than if you had a higher deductible. Lean toward picking the highest deductible that you can afford, and only make claims if there is significant damage to your car or home. You want the insurance company to see you as a good risk and charge you less for insurance.

STEP 5: REVIEW HEALTH INSURANCE PROVISIONS AND FOLLOW THE RULES OF YOUR HEALTH PLAN CAREFULLY.

Most health insurance is selected during an open enrollment period toward the end of the year. You can also make changes to your health insurance if you have a "life event," such as getting married, getting divorced, having a child, or retiring. Open enrollment is a great time to make sure you fully understand the terms of your health insurance plan. If you have a choice of various high deductible plans, be careful when choosing the deductible amount, as these plans can be expensive. As discussed in chapter ten, "Commonsense Ways to Save on Your Health Insurance," there are ways to make sure you are getting as much as possible from your health insurance.

Under current law, insurance companies cannot charge you more if you are sick or have some other health condition. Therefore, making fewer claims will not change the overall premium you are charged but will change how much you pay overall due to deductibles and copayments. Throughout the year, regularly review how much of your deductible you have satisfied, as if you've paid the entire deductible, it will be cheaper to get medical services in the current year than waiting until the next plan year.

Step 6: Identify insurance products you don't need. and take action

If you have insurance that you do not need, consider getting rid of the policy. My stepfather had a life insurance policy that he purchased over twenty-five years ago. He didn't need the insurance, but since he had been paying for it for so long, he wondered if he should just continue paying. After looking at his last policy statement, he learned that the insurance had a good deal of cash value, meaning he would get some money from the insurance company if he surrendered the policy. The decision was difficult for him, as he had paid so much in premiums over the years, and, if he surrendered the policy, he would never collect on the insurance. But after we talked, he understood that the insurance protected him when he needed it, and, since he no longer needs it, he decided to stop paying for it and get the cash value.

Final Step: Enjoy your life

We cannot eliminate all risk from our lives, and, unfortunately, every day bad things happen to good people. However, insurance products allow us to live our lives while being financially protected if something bad happens. I hope being fully protected provides you with peace of mind so you can enjoy your life to the fullest extent possible. I appreciate the time you have spent reading this book and wish you the best in the future.

GLOSSARY OF THE COMMON INSURANCE TERMS USED IN THIS BOOK

The bold terms used in this book are defined below for your reference. The definition is the meaning of the words in an insurance context and will not include other, noninsurance uses of the words.

Account value: Account value is the amount of money in an insurance or annuity policy. The account value is not necessarily the amount of money the policy owner will receive if he or she surrenders or cancels the policy. That is the cash value (see definition below).

Beneficiary: The beneficiary is the person who receives the money from a life insurance policy when the person who the insurance covers dies.

Bonus interest rate or bonus payment: A bonus interest rate is a temporary, higher than market interest rate paid on a deferred annuity or a cash-value life insurance policy. A bonus payment is an extra amount credited to the account value of a deferred annuity, usually on a one-time basis. Both of these items are marketing gimmicks and are not "free money."

Captive insurance agent: Captive insurance agents sell products from one insurance company (and its affiliated companies) only.

Cash value: The cash value of an insurance or annuity policy is the amount of money the policy owner could receive if he or she surrenders or cancels the policy. Often, the cash value equals the account value less a surrender charge.

Cash-value life insurance: Some life insurance policies with cash value are marketed as savings products because they provide both life insurance protection plus a savings/investment element. Cash-value life insurance includes traditional whole life and universal life products.

Certain period: The time period during which annuity payments are guaranteed to be made, even if the person receiving the annuity payments dies. A certain period is often part of an income annuity that has a lifetime guarantee.

Coinsurance: Coinsurance is often shown as a percentage and represents the amount the person with the insurance is responsible for paying. For example, a coinsurance percentage of 30 percentage means that the insurance company pays for only 70 percent of the approved claim amount.

Commission: A commission is a payment made to a person who sells an insurance product. It is how many insurance agents get paid for doing their jobs.

Copayment: A copayment (often called a "copay") is a dollar amount that the person with the insurance is responsible for paying when receiving a service covered by insurance. Copays are common in health insurance.

Coverage limit: See limit.

Deductible: A deductible is the amount the person with the insurance is responsible for paying when there is a claim. Deductibles are common on car, homeowner's, and health insurance.

Deferral of taxation: Interest earned on most insurance and annuity policies is not taxed immediately but is taxed only when money is taken out of the policy. This is a valuable benefit.

Deferred annuity: A deferred annuity is a type of annuity used to save for retirement. Although it's called an annuity, most people don't use a deferred annuity to generate regular (monthly) income payments.

Deferred lifetime income annuity: An income annuity provides regular (monthly) income payments. A lifetime income annuity pays those income payments while the person who the annuity covers is alive (i.e., the payments stop when the person dies). In a deferred lifetime income annuity, the payments start in a number of years (e.g., fifteen years) in the future.

Defined-benefit retirement plan: Historically, pension plans would pay a certain amount of one's salary prior to retirement (e.g., 60 percent) as retirement income for life. Since these plans had a specific amount of benefit, they are often called a defined-benefit retirement plans.

Defined-contribution retirement plan: Employers deposit a certain amount of money into a defined-contribution retirement plan, and the employees use this money to generate income in retirement. No specific benefit amount is guaranteed. Individual and Roth IRAs and 401(k) and 403(b) plans are examples of defined-contribution retirement plans.

Endorsement: See rider.

Equity-indexed annuity: See fixed-indexed annuity.

Exclusion: Something that is not covered under your insurance policy.

Fixed-indexed annuity: A fixed-indexed annuity is a type of deferred annuity in which the interest earned on the policy is determined based on the increase in a particular stock market index (i.e., the S&P 500).

Flexible premium deferred annuity (FPDA): An FPDA is similar to a single premium deferred annuity (SPDA), but the FPDA allows multiple deposits into the policy, where the SPDA allows only one.

Guaranteed issue: Guaranteed issue insurance can be purchased with "no questions asked." Often, benefits under the policy are limited if the insurance is needed soon after purchase.

High-risk pool: Insurance for people who have a large risk of loss may have to purchase insurance from a high-risk pool. This type of insurance is usually expensive, although the cost may be subsidized by the government in some circumstances.

Illustration: An illustration is a hypothetical projection of an insurance or annuity policy's value in the future. The illustration often shows a guaranteed value, based on the minimum guarantees in the policy and another larger value (which can have various names) that is based on more favorable assumptions to the owner of the policy. The illustration shows how the policy will work *only if those particular assumptions actually occur in the future*.

Immediate lifetime income annuity: An income annuity provides regular (monthly) income payments. A lifetime income annuity pays those income payments while the person who the annuity covers is alive (i.e., the payments stop when the person dies). In an immediate lifetime income annuity, the payments start soon after the annuity is purchased.

Income annuity: See deferred lifetime income annuity and immediate lifetime income annuity.

Independent insurance agent: Independent insurance agents sell products from multiple insurance companies.

Indexed annuity: See fixed-indexed annuity.

Inflation: The increase in the price of things is called inflation.

Joint-life lifetime income annuity: Sometimes called a joint and last survivor annuity. A joint-life annuity will make payments when either of two people (often spouses) is alive. Some joint-life annuities will decrease the annuity payment when one of the people dies. Common payments after the death of one person are 75 or 50 percent of the benefit when both people are alive.

Juvenile life insurance: Life insurance where a child is the person being insured.

Life expectancy: The average expected future lifetime. A life expectancy is for people in average health, and, in general, the life expectancy for a woman is longer than for a man.

Limited underwriting: Insurance sold with limited underwriting is similar to guaranteed issue, but only a few questions are asked.

Limit: A coverage limit in car, homeowner's, or liability insurance is the maximum amount the policy will pay if there is a claim.

Longevity insurance: See deferred lifetime income annuity. A deferred lifetime income annuity can also be called longevity insurance.

Market value adjustment (MVA): A type of surrender charge on a deferred annuity, computed using a formula that takes into account the level of interest rates and the remaining time the deferred annuity has until to the end of the interest rate guaranteed period. The MVA will decrease the surrender value if interest rates have increased. It also may increase the surrender value if interest rates have decreased on some deferred annuity policies. See the terms of the policy for more information.

Policy loan: A policy loan is an option on a cash-value life insurance policy in which the owner of the policy can access a portion of the account value without canceling the policy. A policy loan is similar to borrowing a portion of the policy's value, as the loan increases with interest. If a policy loan is equal to the value in the policy, the policy will terminate without value unless some of the policy loan is repaid.

Qualified annuity: Money that has not been taxed by the federal government is called qualified money. An example of qualified money would be money in a 401(k) plan or an individual retirement account (IRA). A qualified annuity is an annuity (usually a deferred annuity) that is purchased using qualified money.

Rider: A rider is an optional extra part of an insurance policy or an annuity that adds some feature or guarantee. A rider always increases the cost of the policy even if the additional cost is not explicitly shown.

Single premium deferred annuity (SPDA): An SPDA is an annuity product sold by an insurance company that is used to grow retirement savings. Money deposited increases with interest and decreases due to charges and fees.

Surrender charge: The surrender charge is an amount charged by the insurance company that decreases the amount of money received when money is taken out of an insurance or annuity policy. The account value less the surrender charge is the cash value of the policy.

Tax deferral: See deferral of taxation.

Term life insurance: Term life insurance is life insurance that is designed to stay in place for a limited time. In most term life policies, the premium is guaranteed to be the same for a number of years, specified at the time of purchase. After the initial guarantee period ends, the premium often significantly increases. Most people cancel the policy at that time (or just stop paying the premium) and purchase a new policy if the life insurance is still needed.

Umbrella liability policy: An umbrella liability policy pays for financial payments required to be made from a covered event by the insured person in excess of car and homeowner's insurance liability limits, up to the limit of the umbrella policy.

Underwriting: When an insurance company asks questions and gathers other information about the risk being insured, it is called underwriting. Insurance companies underwrite to determine how much to charge to cover the risk.

Variable annuity: A variable annuity is a type of deferred annuity in which the interest earned in the policy is determined based on the performance of mutual funds selected by the owner of the annuity.

Whole life insurance: Whole life insurance is a life insurance policy designed to be in place for the lifetime of the insured person. It is sometimes called "permanent" life insurance as it is designed to remain in place until a person dies. Whole life insurance policies often have a cash value. The most popular types of whole life insurance are called "traditional life" and "universal life."

Acknowledgements

I WANT TO THANK MY wife, Edwina, for being so supportive of me in general and this project in particular. I appreciate your encouragement when I needed it the most and your understanding when I spent all those hours in front of the computer working on this book. As with many things in my life, I could not have done this without you!

A huge thank you to Mike Angelina, Andy Erkis, Ron Erkis, Karen Grote, Sandy Jenkins and Dave Neve who read draft versions of my work and provided comments, suggestions and insights that made the book so much better.

Finally, I want to thank Greta Dzedzy whose wonderful artwork graces the cover. Thank you for your patience working with me on the many drawings it took to get this done. You are quite a talent.

Author Biography

Todd Erkis is an actuary and former insurance executive who worked in the industry for over twenty-five years. He understands how insurance works from the inside. Several years ago, Mr. Erkis stepped away from his insurance role to teach finance and risk management at St. Joseph's University in Philadelphia, Pennsylvania.

With a wife and three children, he has had to navigate the challenging world of purchasing insurance himself and knows how hard it is to get a good deal. He will use his expert knowledge and personal experience to teach you how to get the insurance protection you need.

www.ingramcontent.com/pod-product-compliance
Lightning Source LLC
Chambersburg PA
CBHW071435180526
45170CB00001B/351